Every Face Has a

Story...

D1607307

True Stories of Hope & Difficulties

from Venezuelan Immigrants

Dr. Dale Olson

Julie Ostos, Illustrator

I dedicate this book to all my Venezuelan friends and my dear wife, Alene, who is my soulmate and best friend.

4

Contents

6

INTRODUCTION

The phrase, *"Diamonds in the Rough,"* projects a passion to discover more than the eye first can see. Imagine that you live somewhere in the world where you have become obsessed with diamonds. As you seek to become richer, your dreams consume you in finding a large field of "diamonds in the rough." So, you travel to parts of the world seeking amazing, beautiful diamonds that will make you rich. One day, you are at home taking a rest from your travels, and you are walking your dog in the field. You notice a unique, large protruding black rock sticking up out of the ground. Your first impulse is to sigh and say to yourself, "One more big rock to remove from this field!" Then you take one more look at this ordinary rock. Upon closer examination, you begin to look at the face of the rock more carefully. In all your obsession with diamonds, you wonder: Could this really be a diamond? After you call the diamond experts, the result is one of the largest diamonds ever found, and to your surprise and joy, your whole field is full of diamonds!

Do you know any immigrants? If so, would you consider them like diamonds? In your mind, do you lump all immigrants together, implying they are all the same? Before meeting them, you may draw some immediate conclusions and wonder: Where are they from? Did they come here legally or illegally? Do any family members speak English? Do they have any higher education degrees? Do they have jobs? What is their story? In my experience, I have knocked on their doors and welcomed new immigrant families from many countries. Although they were often embarrassed by the lack of perfect English, the Venezuelans surprised me by their education and work skills. In this collection of stories from Venezuelans, may you discover that every face has a story of hope and challenges. You will learn firsthand from Venezuelans as they recount their life and death experiences.

As CEO of a non-profit organization in Fort Bend County, Texas, I met people from all over the world. When you asked the question in Fort Bend County, "Where are you from?" the answer might be any number of countries including India, Russia, Cuba, Peru, Honduras, Afghanistan, Columbia, Venezuela, and others because it is one of the most diverse counties in the U.S. Similarly, when our organization hosted monthly food fairs to provide food to families in need, you would hear many languages spoken along with the cultures of Asian, African American, Hispanic and Caucasian. I insisted we treat all people with dignity, and all were served an equal amount of food. As I began to see some of the same faces month after month, I began to hear the unique stories of one group of people making their journey from Venezuela to Miami and then to Katy, Texas.

Where did I first really get to know the Venezuelan? I came to hear of the plight of Venezuelans when Family Hope offered an ESL class for those new to the U.S. Eight couples and four single moms attended these classes...all immigrants from Venezuela. Today in the heated political battles of border crossings, words like "immigrants" and "refugees" are buzz words that often shout out ILLEGAL! As I began to listen to these families, I discovered the Venezuelans did not fit into these stereotypes. These Venezuelan families had a passion in their eyes to learn English because they knew fluent English meant a better job so their families could prosper. In their previous life in Venezuela, they knew the value of hard work and lived a good life. In the past, they rose to respectable positions of authority in their jobs and even travelled to the U.S. for family vacations. They loved Venezuela, but they spoke about their beautiful country steadily eroding by a Marxist government, intent on replacing oil production with drug trafficking. As a result, in a matter of only a few years, Venezuela evolved from one of the richest countries in their area of the globe to one of the poorest. For example, I know a medical student who will soon be a licensed doctor. When he graduates, his salary will be $30/month if he chooses to practice in Venezuela. Where will this young person go to receive better compensation for his skills? Highly educated business leaders realized the present regime was giving the people empty promises and bankrupting their beloved country. As a result, they waited patiently until it was the right time to begin a new life in America. This is the "brain-drain" that is happening.

How did I come to collect these Venezuelans stories? Nine years ago, I was asked by the community leaders of Fulshear and Simonton, Texas to start and lead an emergency relief organization called Family Hope. The vision was to provide emergency assistance for food, rent, and emergency medical needs, while at the same time, giving them resources to improve their lives and potentially connect them to a job. I collaborated with government, civic, business and church leaders to serve our new neighbors and give them a path to succeed in America. As a CEO of this new 501 c3 organization, the sign read on the door, "All are welcome!" By the end of 2022, Family Hope served over 42,000 individuals with food each year. Over half of the families served were Venezuelans. Thus, the following pages are devoted to a glimpse into the stories of our new neighbors, the Venezuelans, who experienced tragedy, heartache, loss, persecution and now hope coming to America. May you feel like you are walking in their shoes as you read their stories about leasing their first apartment in America with very minimal resources and wondering if they would "make it in America."

I share this collection because I believe the stories of Venezuelans have not been told. When I would visit friends and relatives living in other regions of the U.S., I would explain what I had learned from these new Venezuelan immigrants coming to America. I would describe the unique DNA of Venezuelans. I would tell stories about doctors, lawyers, business owners as well as moms and dads willing to work any job to succeed in America. Most friends and relatives reacted with surprise.

As our staff and I made it a priority to welcome and show dignity to the Venezuelans, the Venezuelans, in turn, lovingly gave me a nickname, *Mr. Hope.* I wore that name as a badge of honor as I continued to find great joy in extending hope to these kind people. Every week, the Family Hope truck would be seen bringing food to those in need…bringing a bed and table to their apartment so they no longer had to sleep on the floor…providing help with rent so they would not be evicted. It is true that love is contagious! The community of northern Fort Bend County caught the spirit and returned the kindness to the Venezuelans. It became a whole community effort to find ways to serve the Venezuelans and help them find jobs. I am grateful for the business community, individual donors and churches who invested in the Venezuelan future with their generous gifts.

My life and heart have been blessed by listening to the stories of Venezuelans. As I reread the collection of stories, I am in awe of the Venezuelans who risked their lives leaving Venezuela. They had to abandon their businesses and homes, leave their parents and cousins in Venezuela, and start over in America. All the stories have only a first name to protect their identity. Also, you will discover that some stories intentionally omit details of their journeys from Venezuela to America because they still fear the Venezuelan authorities. I pray you will feel their tears and determination in this new land. I hope their stories inspire you to appreciate the value that Venezuelans bring to America.

11

CHAPTER ONE

Facing Difficulties

Rubi

My story begins while working in a very high office of the government in Venezuela as the Executive Director for an agency related to the Supreme Court. In this government agency, all the workers were ordered by the governor to march outside to support his causes. We were forced to attend these marches even if we disagreed with the government's regime. I began to worry when I heard of workers being threatened with survival if you disobeyed any of these orders or did not show up for work on these days. I was already feeling the economic squeeze of inflation eating up our profits and salaries. Since I was one of them who never agreed to support the government's regime in any march, I began to be threatened on various occasions. Often people in charge of the logistics for the marches and supporters of the government expected all of us to leave work early, and they would throw tear gas bombs at four of my colleagues who didn't agree with the regime. By mid-2016, many people who were peacefully calling for a change of leadership in the country had been murdered. Each time I left the office from work, I had to look for my two-year old daughter and pick her up from the nursery and under the protests and in the midst of the line of fire of the violence. My daughter and I had to wear damp handkerchiefs to prevent us from inhaling the gas bombs fumes. My sadness came when a co-worker, whom I dearly respected, was murdered by the government for disagreeing with its policies. Finally, the next day, I resigned from my position with the government and tried to keep hidden until I could flee the country. I shared this news about my co-worker with my husband, and he was very disturbed about the injustice and violence by the government. Soon this violence became more personal. One morning, my husband set out for work, and he was intercepted by government officials and murdered. They went to our house and wrote on the walls that no one else dares to live if they are opposed to the government. That day our lives changed! I was devastated! I knew my life was gaining more value, and I had to protect myself in order to take care of our daughter. I stayed two more years in hiding until I could leave the country.

I was terrified for both my daughter and me. I couldn't leave with a two-year old. Finally, a cousin supported me in receiving me in Panama for a month. Then I prepared my travels to Mexico as a tourist to learn about the opportunities to save my life, look for work and start a new life together with my family. I remember I had to move several times for security reasons as I would try to hire lawyers and obtain a work permit. During this time, my daughter received safe keeping in Venezuela until we could be reunited. Mexico ended up being dangerous when my daughter finally was able to join me in Mexico. I lived in Mexico for five years, and I am grateful for a family to share their home with me.

When I look back, I thought I was lucky to be born in such prosperous country as Venezuela, but unfortunately, I saw them take away the pillar of my family, my husband, and all I had achieved in my career. Finally, I decided to cross the border to the United States. We needed a better life. It has not been easy. I do jobs of cleaning and cooking, but I am grateful to St. Faustina Church and Gledys at Family Hope for their generous hearts. Today, I trust in God and the angels and the good safe system of order in the U.S. It is a safe country for both of us where we still have more opportunities to live without persecution and live a healthy, safe life with dignity. I feel sad because I will never see my father and my mother again. I have discovered the U.S. is a big country with lots of opportunities and people with generous hearts. My daughter can grow old in this country with lots of opportunity and a safe place. My daughter's school has surpassed all expectations. She speaks English and Spanish, and now she is learning Chinese. I made the right decision to come to America…a land of opportunity and freedom…to be all that we want to be. Thanks to God for bringing me this far!

Gledys

This country has been wonderful to us. It is filled with lots of opportunities. In Venezuela, I received a degree in Administration…Pharmacy Assistant.

In 2011, my husband applied for a visa through the lottery program in Venezuela. Five years later in 2017, he received notice that he now could go to the United States. He asked me, "Gledys, do you want to go to the U.S?" I quickly responded, "I love my country." But eventually, our once beautiful country was being destroyed by our leaders.

In 2016, we had an interview with the American Embassy. We decided to celebrate every day as if it would be our last day here, not knowing the date nor the hour that we would leave. My husband was a good and successful businessman. He provided income for four families. I remember crying many days after the reality that we would need to take the big step to leave our country. We began filling out documents including medical information, marriage license and background check.

I remember the day we left in 2017. We flew to Miami and then to Houston. I had a friend in Katy, TX. My husband hired a person to make a lease contract, and within two days, we were in our first apartment in the U.S. We spent about $10,000 to get our life set up with an apartment and car. After that week, we only had $6,000 left since we had to leave the entire business behind in Venezuela. Initially, three organizations really helped us. The Church of Christ congregation, KCM and Family Hope. On Sundays, we would attend church and we would receive food which really helped. During the first month in Texas, I was so scared. I thought people would frown upon us and reject us because we didn't speak English. But I quickly met Christians and so many people who opened their arms to us to help.

A year later, we attended an ESL class by Family Hope. This changed everything for us! We met Mr. Dale (Dale Olson), who has become an angel to the Venezuelan community. There were twelve families in the class from Venezuela. We have stayed in touch with each other and have become good friends as we make our life in America. Eventually, I would have my first employment at Family Hope. I feel so blessed!

I feel very sad for my country. The people now arriving from Venezuela do not have the same level of education that we did. Remember, Venezuela was once a country where people from all over the world came to live and enjoy our beautiful life. Now it is a "Brain-Drain" of educated and professional businesspeople who are fleeing from the country.

Three decisions have impacted me the most in America. 1. As I said, I attended my first ESL class sponsored by Family Hope. This began friendships and my relationship to Family Hope. I realize now how important English is to make it in America. Now I tell all the new Venezuelans, "Learn English as quickly as you can." 2. My kids attending school has forced me to become acquainted with the school environment and my neighbors. I feel like I am part of the neighborhood. 3. Being on staff with Family Hope. Today, I am the one who connects these four hundred Venezuelan families with resources and information given by Family Hope. This is my dream job to help Venezuelans and others seeking assistance. I feel so blessed to work and be a friend with Mr. Dale, who we call "Mr. Hope."

Every day I have the opportunity to hear the stories of Venezuelans coming here in their first week or month of life in America. One day when Mr. Dale asked me why I was so tired, I told him: "I have been cleaning houses because I want to experience what other Venezuelan women are doing." I tell migrants that the first six months will be tough. But keep your faith and have courage to adjust to this transition. Many doors will open in America. This is the greatest country in the world. I feel so sad for my home country, Venezuela, and how the leaders have betrayed the people. When I hear of our own U.S. government thinking about buying oil from Venezuela, I say to myself, "Why, do you want to make a deal with the Devil? The money will not make it to the people. It will only be used for drugs and prostitution.

Recently, on the day of being approved for citizenship in the U.S., I am now an American citizen wherever I stand. I am very proud to be an American citizen. I feel now that I have roots. I look back at these past five years, and it has been an evolution for our family. What if we had stayed? Life would have become worse. We do not know what the Venezuela government would have done to threaten our business and quality of life. Today, I make people happy by my baking and with my position at Family Hope. I know I touch many lives. We bought a house a year ago. And we feel safe in our neighborhood. Today, I want to "pay it forward" by helping others who come to America. The United States of America is a beautiful country…a place of many opportunities. Sometimes Americans forget how this land is so filled with opportunities. Just like when we were preparing to leave Venezuela and treasuring every day, I wake up in the morning to say, "Thank you, God, for this day and for this country. I feel so blessed! Give me an opportunity to be a good neighbor."

Chacon

I left Venezuela with my husband and two children in 2019. It was a very difficult time for us. I remember the day the government closed the airport, and we had to cross the border of Colombia riding motorcycles. After a long journey, we managed to take a plane that would take us to our new destiny. In looking back, the Venezuelan regime tried to silence our voices for not agreeing with the dictatorship. Certainly, we saw many of our friends and neighbors killed in an attempt to recover Democracy. From the hearts of a military family, my parents always gave the example of doing things well and abiding by the constitution of the country and not giving into the regime's corrupt ways. Out of fear and desperation for a better life, we wished to live in a free country where with perseverance and dedication, we can achieve our goals. As engineers, we were determined to make this a new day for our family.

After a long journey, we arrived in the U.S. eager to start a new life. We spent the first few days in Florida at the home of some relatives. We are so grateful for their advice and warm hospitality. But we were focused on coming to Texas. Two weeks later, we arrived in Houston, hoping to start our lives in this beautiful city, specifically in Katy, where great friends opened the doors of their house to us to welcome us. Finally, with the help of cousins and friends, we moved into an apartment with our hopes and fears. Our children began to study in their schools. By May 2022, both of our children finished their high school courses. It was such an emotional time for us to see our children succeed in America. All the sacrifices have been worth it!

We have worked hard with determination and perseverance, always focusing on doing things with excellence. We are so grateful for this free country, giving us endless opportunities. We feel so blessed to be here and meet wonderful people with big hearts. One of the people who blessed us was Gledys from Family Hope. I am so grateful for her support and for giving me a helping hand. How do I describe Gledys and her workers? Humility and a big heart! Thanks for blessing our lives as we begin a new future in America!

Gledys N.

I was a group insurance executive in Venezuela. When I saw my country decline in economics and values, I decided to come to America. I wanted to improve the quality of education for our children, culturally, socially, and offer growth in opportunities to succeed.

At first the language was the most difficult to overcome. My husband had only $80 when he began his two jobs in America at a paint store and at night in a pizzeria. Our first intention was to earn enough money to move to Europe. However, after five months in the U.S., our plans changed. We want to stay in America filled with opportunities though we miss our family in Venezuela.

We are grateful to church groups for helping us with food and diapers. I think back to when we first came to America and how we lived in a small apartment with one bedroom for four people for almost four years. But we never gave up on our dreams. They say in America that you can dream big. We are now living that dream. We own our own house, and my husband has created a fiber optic company, which he founded with his partner two years ago. Now our daughters are five and six years old and we have a baby on the way. Some days we wonder how we have made it this far. Then we realize that it has all been possible because of God who provided the stones along the road to walk on to achieve our goals. It is so good to be in America!

Sikiu Millan

I am 47 years old from Venezuela and married with two teenage children, 15 and 13. In Venezuela, I worked as a Cost Estimation Manager in a State-run company. However, I experienced workplace and personal harassment because I did not share the same political position as the company leaders. I felt that my life and my family were at risk, so I decided to immigrate to the U.S. in 2021. I left the rest of my family behind including my grandmother, my house, and friends so I could protect my children in America.

I remember the day I arrived in America with one suitcase and four backpacks. All sorts of feelings were swimming in my mind...fear, sadness, confusion, and emptiness in our hearts as we wondered what it would mean to start our lives over in America. Even the climate was new to us. Cold invaded our bones, and we wondered how we would ever get ahead financially at our age. With a new language and $200 for food, we prayed that God would show mercy on us. One day, as I was talking to a neighbor, she told me about Family Hope and the possible help for me. Right then, I decided to go to Family Hope Food Fair where volunteers were passing out food to everyone. It was there, I met Rosangela, who extended her hand to me. I felt I found a part of Venezuela in her, and for the first time, I had hope that we would survive. We were not alone. Mrs. Rosangela invited us to go to the Family Hope office, and there I met a generous kind man, Mr. Dale, who radiated like a father to us and even made our nervous scared son feel loved. As Mr. Dale visited with us, he realized that our apartment was not furnished so we were sleeping on inflatable mattresses. In just a few days, the Family Hope truck pulled up in front of our apartment to bring beds for our children, my husband and me as well as a dining room table and kitchen items. We had so many tears of happiness that day! In the coming weeks, Family Hope did not forget about us but supplied us with food, Christmas gifts for my children and so many blessings of love. Thanks to Jehovah God, we are now feeling better and more stable after 15 months in the U.S. I am now developing a business…thanks to the Family Hope team. I feel so blessed as God sent these wonderful people into my life!

Monica

I arrived in the U.S. in October 2019 with a suitcase full of dreams, hopes and a lot of faith. Yet I had a wrinkled heart full of sadness and eyes swollen with tears that seemed not to stop. I had never had to say "Good-bye" to my parents, my relatives, friends, businesses, home and endless things, small or not, and as a result, the experience produced a huge void in my heart and soul. Less than a year in the U.S., I received several voice messages, but without audio, which indicated a bad omen was coming. Finally, my brother managed to gain courage and tell me my mother had died. My world seemed to fall apart. When I left Venezuela, I knew I never would see her again, but now I had such sadness that I could not even say goodbye or give her one last hug. 22 days later, my sister and I received a call from my nephew to tell us that my father had died of a heart attack. I am sure that he died with a broken heart as he missed my mother. Certainly, moving on from these losses is possible, but a part of you dies in the process. I can't write this without tears running down my cheeks.

God's timing is perfect because amidst the sadness, Family Hope appeared at the right time. In 2021, my nephew was diagnosed with COVID-19. He needed oxygen, medications, gasoline and transportation. In short, this was a time when our resources ran out and yet there was an Angel on the way…Family Hope.

After my nephew lost his battle with COVID, Family Hope came to our door to bring diapers for my disabled niece and other food donations that we so needed. It was a miracle that kept us living and believing.

It hasn't been easy. The deaths in our family have been so difficult to handle. But my heart is part of this great family in America who has shown us so much love. We are a grateful family to be here.

Maria B

I worked for 20 years at a company of public accountants in Venezuela dedicated to the collections of municipal taxes. The main reason I came to America was to seek a cure for my son who had been suffering from a medical condition for three years. In Venezuela, he had been treated by more than 25 specialists without any improvement. In America, we found the needed care that we were seeking. Slowly my son improved. Certainly, the language and customs were a barrier for us to live, but the saddest part was missing my family and the businesses we worked at for years.

Today, we are here thanks to the charity of many people and the discovery of new talents and opportunities for us. I believe God sent angels along the way to assist my family. My greatest joy is to see my son healthy, safe and happy with a bright future full of opportunities for him and us. I am now becoming better at English. My husband and I are both advancing in our jobs and are receiving approvals for our immigration process. I feel no longer alone, but so grateful.

Centeno

My husband and I met at the university in Venezuela. We studied together with sociology and law degrees. We remember the beautiful ceremony where we both received our degrees. We treasure that time!

For a while, we lived well. I worked for five years as a legal representative of a company and my husband began a company. Suddenly, everything started getting worse…the insecurity in the country, the scarcity of food and the blackouts of electricity which often lasted nine days. Finally, the blackouts made us decide to immigrate.

When we arrived in Texas, we had many friends who told us that the schools were excellent. This was a priority for our daughter. In 2019, I worked as a waitress and my husband in construction. We were happy although we had no mattress to sleep on nor a table and chairs to sit and eat. In December, I discovered that I was pregnant with twins, which was really a shock to us. At the same time, we had gratitude to God because we had been trying to have a second child for two years. During that time, I had five miscarriages, something that left us devastated. Today, we are thankful to God for our children. We both have work and good health. It has not been easy, but we have each other, and God is with us. I tell all the new people coming from Venezuela: "Don't lose your faith. God is with you!"

Elivir

I was born in beautiful Venezuela. I earned a master's degree in architecture. In Venezuela, I served as a specialist in Real Estate Appraisal and in the Procurement of Materials for the construction sector. Originally, we came to America for a vacation. As a result, we decided to stay for the future of my son. I am a single mother, and my son is 14 years old.

Like all immigrants, my first few months in America were so difficult though I was very fortunate to have three sisters living here for the past 15 years. The most difficult was to start over from nothing. A new land and a new language become so overwhelming at times. However, I have witnessed three places of compassion during this difficult time: Family Hope, St. Faustina Church, and Epiphany Church.

Now after five years in the U.S., I am beginning to see a light at the end of the tunnel. I now have a job in the school district, I believe there is a great future for my son.

Vilchez

We arrived in this country in 2021 with the help of relatives of my husband. We have two children. My husband worked in the oil industry as an Analyst for the purchase and sale of materials. I am a nurse. Also, I have skills in hair styling and in baking.

The separation from our family and friends was very difficult for us including leaving my husband's aging mother in Venezuela since she does not have an American visa. We left all our household belongings in Venezuela in exchange for a better future for our children. Another reason that we decided to come to America is health treatment for our son since he suffers from heart failure. It was too risky to rely on the Venezuelan medical treatments since the medical supplies are often in short supply.

The first few months were difficult but provided great hope by family and friends who directed us to Family Hope as well as churches to receive help with rent and food. As we wait for our case of Political Asylum to be approved, God continues to be our source of strength. Along with the family separation, we worry about the timing of our legal status. When will our Political Asylum be approved? On the other hand, I have witnessed a great miracle in this country. Through God and the medicine in this country, my sister has been able to overcome cancer. All of us are so filled with joy and thanksgiving to God for this healing.

Today, our children are safe in this new country, and we are so grateful. Thank you, Family Hope, for helping us make a new home in America.

REFLECTIONS: Facing Difficulties

In another generation, my great grandfather decided to board a ship in Sweden to begin a new life in America. The day before he boarded the ship, he stopped to see his girlfriend although he was aware he had competition because another man was courting her too, a richer man than he. During the conversation, he invited her to come down to the docks and see him off the next day, or even better, come with him and join him in this new venture to America. Within 24 hours, she met him at the docks and to his surprise, she made a bold decision with her suitcase in hand to wave goodbye together to the only home they knew. Many years later after homesteading a home in America, clearing land and planting rows of crops, my great grandmother said, "Some days I was surprised we survived. Life has not been easy." Along with learning English and becoming acquainted with a new culture, my great grandparents as immigrants created an amazing life of family, work and faith. Both would say despite all the hard work and difficulties, it was worth it. To this day, I am grateful and stand in awe of them for birthing our family and new healthy traditions in America.

Today, Venezuelans come to America and speak similar words, "It has not been easy." They usually fly legally to Miami and then make their home in places like Houston or more dangerously come across the Border, and settle in Katy, Texas. In their new community, they lease an apartment, find jobs, and enroll their children in schools. In the past, many were required to follow an outdated U.S. law that forbid them to work for the first five months. Whether they come with master's or doctorate degrees, they are eager to find any job they can to support their family.

These new jobs will not be equivalent to the ones back in Venezuela. To be certified as a doctor will take many years of study to attain their new degree in America. For some, they will acquire new skills to succeed. Like my great grandparents, to make their way in this new country, it will be essential to learn English and find ways to fit into the culture. Already, I have heard their children repeat the same gratefulness as I have for my great grandparents, "I am so glad my parents took the risk for a better life in America!" The birthing of a new life in America is already reaping amazing benefits and creating new and healthy family traditions. These faces with a story of hope and grit are the future for America. However, all of them will need to persevere as they face immense difficulties. Life will not be easy!

We do not have to be immigrants to face difficulties. When I listen to the stories of those who were born in America as well as new immigrants living here for only a few months, I hear about the difficulties of broken relationships and lack of adequate income to support their families. Some children and adults wear scars from their past that create a series of brokenness. On the other hand, some grieve a child or parent's action that they no longer can control. Most Venezuelans I met came to Family Hope because they needed more food for their family, or they just could not pay their rent and were facing eviction. All these feelings created an anxiety that their world was spinning out of control. For that purpose, God has set us in community because people need people! We need one another to help us get through the tough days. Even the images of our brain looks healthier when we have a nurturing community around us. We need organizations like Family Hope, which bring us compassion in the face of hurt. We need God to be our strength in weakness. I have discovered the life we wish for is not the absence of difficulties and tough times, but our daily determination to believe God will provide us with enough strength for the moment, "I can do all things through Him who strengthens me." (Philippians 4:13 NASB)

Educators and therapists have discovered that lives shielded from life's hurts and obstacles do not always build the needed "grit" we need in life to tackle the daily difficulties. Sometimes when children are given too much by their parents or not challenged enough will sometimes develop a pattern of either quitting or skipping the needed steps when life gets tough. Just like building muscles, we build strength as we deal with the brokenness of our world. "Consider it all joy, my brethren, when you encounter various trials, knowing that testing of your faith produces endurance. And let endurance have its perfect result, so that you may be perfect and complete, lacking in nothing." (James 1:2-4 NASB) Now if you are going through a tough season of life, no one wants to be told, "All these problems will make you stronger and better." However, endurance pays off! My son recently told me, "Dad, these days I want to listen to the speakers who have gone through some pain. They are the ones I want to learn from." If you are going through a tough season, do not try to take a short cut from trouble or even quit. Venezuelans experience the same test. Many of them are very intelligent and educated. In fact, most of them were very successful in Venezuela in high positions of authority and overseeing important businesses. Coming to America with minimal English quickly humbles them because they will need a greater pound of fortitude to roll up their sleeves and take jobs they never had to do in Venezuela. As a result, most Venezuelans seem to make the shift very quickly with their determination to succeed in America. Once they have committed themselves to immigration documents in America, they cannot go back to Venezuela so they must survive and find a way to thrive.

In times of facing tough seasons of life, I turn to God who created me and calls me a beloved child. I find it comforting to hear God give Jesus the title "My Beloved Son" when Jesus was baptized by John in the Jordan River. "Immediately coming up out of the water, He saw the heavens opening, and the Spirit like a dove descending upon Him, and a voice came out of the heavens, 'You are My beloved Son, in You I am well pleased.'" (Mark 1:9-11 NASB) Similarly, in our own baptism, we are called "Child of God." The old is washed away and God gives us new life. I remember listening to a man who once was a gang member. The attraction was so compelling to belong to someone, or in this situation, a group. He was willing to commit violence to win their acceptance. His life turned around once he discovered this new life of belonging to God's unconditional love and forgiveness. This same ex-gang member is now pointing others to Jesus' life-giving love. In tough seasons, we experience disappointments, addictions, obsessions, loss of dreams, and broken promises. People and organizations betray us, and yet God picks us up and uses some of God's favorite words for us unconditionally, "You are my son. You are my daughter. I love you. You are forgiven." Living forgiven and in God's grace is better than self-pity or revenge. It is a freeing and a healthy way to live! In a world begging for our allegiance, Jesus tells us we belong to God who loves us unconditionally, and in turn, raises us up to new life in ways we never thought possible!

When Venezuelans come to America, they seek to belong and begin to recreate themselves. Most often, they will not be able to work the same profession as they did in Venezuela. They now live in an apartment rather than a house. Most cannot speak English very well. Without friends and family and the familiar pillars of life around them, they ask, "What is my purpose?" Just like us, their name will not be nailed to their past, but new life has come. As neighbors, we can remind them that God is always with them and working in the most amazing ways to prepare a new future and a new purpose. We are God's beloved children no matter what country we call home.

When I saw the faces in the cars who would come for food at Family Hope's Food Fairs, I was aware of the long hours these people worked at one or two jobs. Their determination would not let them quit and just return to Venezuela. If you were born in America, and wondering how you will make it through a tough season, our Venezuelan neighbors can teach us about grit and determination to succeed. When the Family Hope truck would bring a bed to an apartment of a family who had been sleeping on the floor for weeks or months, I wondered how they endured sleeping like that night after night. They would tell me they had a higher purpose to give back to this new country and trust that God would provide. Like my great grandmother would say, "It was tough, but it was worth it." My thanks to my Venezuelan friends for being our teachers in face of adversity.

QUESTIONS:

1. What difficulties or obstacles are you facing this season of life?
2. How are you being called to let go of past guilt or anger, so you can forgive and discover a new way to live? How does God loving you make a difference in your life?
3. What can you learn from the Venezuelans?

31

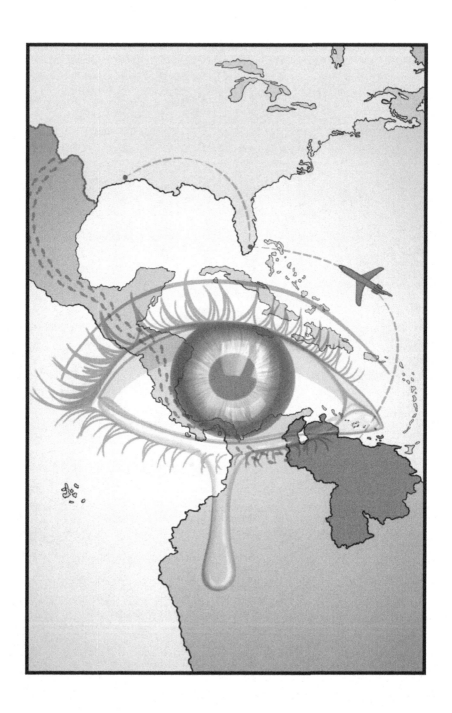

CHAPTER TWO

Fleeing from…Running to…

Henmy

I am 45 years old and married with two children, 10 and 4 years old. I am a Mechanical Engineer with a master's degree in operations management. When I graduated, I applied to a company but was not selected because I had signed a referendum against the government. Since then, my husband and I decided to open a business. Two and a half years later, the government supporters stole our merchandise from our business, forced us to give services for free, and began to threaten us if we did not follow their orders. Finally, we closed our business in 2019 and sold what little was left.

The calls and persecutions by the government continued against our family and neighbors. During the Pandemic, we managed to maintain ourselves, but the situation was already more difficult. Even our children were experiencing danger with threats.

My husband managed to travel to the USA in 2020 since he had a VISA, although the rest of the family did not have those documents. My husband managed to raise enough money to cross the border, a difficult and risky decision. In Venezuela, we lived very hidden since we were not affiliated with the government. Even before we closed our business, we were being persecuted by the evil and cruel regime.

In June, I left Venezuela and crossed the border, passing through high-risk places. The border guards grabbed us and took my children and me to shelters in Phoenix. After leaving the first shelter, they took us to a jail where we stayed for 14 hours. Before they released us from jail, they put a shackle on me. That was a very shocking moment for my children and me. They transferred us to a church in Phoenix where they gave us freedom, and we communicated with my husband so they could pick us up at the airport. Every 15 days, I had to report with a call and every two months a visit at home by migration agents.

Later in June, a friend shared with me about the organization, Family Hope. She gave me the phone numbers of Rosangela and Gledys who treated me with such human warmth and kindness. Thanks to Family Hope for the food that I receive every month. They have helped me pay the rent on my apartment and provided my children with new shoes and school supplies.

Since coming to Texas, Family Hope and its Executive Director, Dr. Dale, have been a blessing to our family. We arrived here with nothing...without clothes, food, or friends. Our only hope was to see my children have a better future and have the right to express themselves freely. This was the most important thing for me.

A thousand thanks for the compassion shown to our entire family. We will never forget the outpouring of love and friendship to us. Thanks. Gratitude and Infinite Faith.

Henry

I came to the U.S. in 2019. I owned a construction business employing over 200 people. As an owner and consultant for 30 years, I loved my work, and we became successful. There was no reason to leave Venezuela. We didn't plan to leave until the birth of our grandson.

We had political problems. I knew people who were supportive of the opposition government. At first, it was a very small political party. But it grew from 100 people to 150,000. Perhaps I was naïve, but I thought that my support was good for the country. However, a leader came to me and said, "The government has seen you and is aware of your political activities."

When I left to visit the U.S., my partner in the business was unexpectedly imprisoned one night. He would be persecuted and tortured in the next few months. In fact, he refuses to ever talk about this very emotional scar.

I ask myself, "How did it get so bad in Venezuela?" The answer is simple: We began electing the wrong leaders who were very corrupt Socialists. The primary purpose of Socialism is to carve out more power for the government. But it is a fine line when power becomes corrupted. If power is in the hands of unethical people, the good intentions are pushed aside for control and abusing individual rights and taking away everyone's freedom. 90% of the people don't want the present government regime. 10% have a thriving business and are living well with huge houses and cars. The rest of the people who are not in the military or government are dying. Today, the government is led by a group of very corrupt and ruthless leaders who prey on the very weak. To complicate the matter, the Russians and Cubans have a big influence upon the government and are draining the resources of the once rich Venezuela.

Someone may ask, "What is the future of Venezuela?" This evolution of a government run by cruel thugs, has been a slow but determined process. 30 years ago, young people experienced a decent living. Today, everyone is in "survival" mode, which changes the ethics and living standard. The quality of education has declined. People cannot write and use the correct grammar. Now, the very educated are leaving in droves which is a "brain-drain" for the country. Therefore, the country is led by people with a lower education. This dictator has affected more than five generations. It makes me sad.

As a result, in November 2020, my wife took the first flight out of Venezuela to an unknown country and finally to Miami. We are very happy in this new country. We have a business, and we feel secure and safe. When I look back, I know we made the right decision to come to America even if we left family and friends behind. We have opportunities for our children. In fact, I know many Venezuelans who are here in America for their children. My father was an immigrant to Venezuela. He saw Venezuela as a "Paradise." I never thought I would be an immigrant in another country.

When I lived in Venezuela, we accepted people from all over the world...Germans, Italians. They came for freedom, liberty and a good life. We appreciated each of their histories. Now we come to America in the same way. Some of us have been scarred by persecution. Some want a better future for our children. But all of us want to be treated with dignity and have the freedom to be what God wants us to be. It takes time to get to know each other. We can be very useful to this country. We are educated and have skills that can add to the success of this great nation.

One thing is sure: We don't want America to become another Venezuela. We love America and say, "Beware. Be careful who you vote for." Protect your nation from ruthless people so in love with power like the corrupt Socialists in Venezuela. They will destroy you. Treasure your history of "For the People" with liberty and freedom.

Jose' S.

It began in year 2014. The situation in my country was getting worse economically, socially, but above all in terms of personal security. The mode of delinquent activity was called "Express Kidnap," which consists in kidnaping high school kids and asking parents for a ransom, or they would never find their child again. Also, I was a Veterinary Doctor in my country and worked at a national referral center for veterinary ophthalmology practice. Although I had the highest level of specialty and all the training, I was just able to charge $1 for a consultation and about $200 for the most expensive surgery. An equivalent surgery in the U.S. would be $5,000. I was becoming professionally discouraged and personally afraid of living in Venezuela. My oldest son was about to graduate from high school in one year and that was the most dangerous age for those "express kidnappings."

My wife and I had a serious conversation and maybe a crazy idea about leaving Venezuela. I did not want to wait until something bad happened to one of our children to decide to leave our country and start a new life elsewhere. I found a program in the state of Texas to become a bilingual certified teacher and obtain a working visa to live in Texas. Since I already was teaching in Venezuela at the university level for 15 years, I felt this plan could work.

I registered for the program, followed all the steps, took all the tests, and finally after one year, I became a bilingual certified teacher for the state of Texas. I participated in a job fair and was hired by one of the largest school districts in Houston to teach 6th grade Math and Science. As a result, I closed my veterinary practice, sold all my veterinary equipment, and came to Texas in July 2015. My wife, our three kids (ages 18, 14, 11) and I came with six suitcases and a big dream of a better future for my children. My wife supported me 100% throughout the process. Without her help, this plan would not have been possible either.

As I started looking for housing, the biggest obstacle was not having a credit history in the U.S. Thankfully, my uncle and godfather lived in Houston and were willing to be co-buyers for a beautiful house. In this way, we started our journey in this new country with an empty house, a car, a few bags of clothes and many dreams.

Today, after 7 years in the U.S., all three of my children are in college through scholarships and grants. Our daughter has decided to walk in her dad's footsteps and train to be a veterinarian. My third child unfortunately was the one having a rough time adapting to this new life. I remember when my son would say, "Dad, let's go back. This is not our country." Fortunately, his girlfriend came to live in Katy, TX so this helped his longing for friends. This transition to a new country caused him to struggle at the university, become depressed and change his major a few times. But thanks be to God, he also found his way and is now in his last year to become a kinesiologist at the university and eventually a Physical Therapist.

As for me, I have been teaching at a public school for eight years. Now I am ready to return to my profession as a veterinarian. I am currently halfway through the process. It hasn't been easy. I needed to study basically my whole career again by myself and with 30 years of updates, changes and with a new language. I am closer every day. I am about to take the national veterinary board exam in a couple of months and then the final practical and clinical examination in about six months.

I especially want to mention the amazing labor in helping people in Venezuela. My wife and I were part of volunteers at a nonprofit organization in Venezuela dedicated to support young women and children with HIV positive. This organization is led by a Catholic Priest in Venezuela. He became a real friend, not to mention a spiritual mentor. When we moved to Texas, he came to visit us and introduced us to a local parish called St. Faustina in Fulshear, TX. The parish decided to help us sponsor the cost of shipping two boxes of food each month to Venezuela. These boxes would feed about 300 elders, women and children each Friday. We began spreading the word among the neighbors and friends about this urgent need. This evolved into another group called Pounds of Love to help parishes in Venezuela. Thus, little by little, these ideas started to grow. We gather the food our house or garage and pack it once a week to be shipped to Venezuela. One day we met Mr. Dale, and now we are part of a larger organization called Family Hope. With their support, we started growing from 2 to 4 to 8 and 16 boxes of food a month sent to six different parishes in Venezuela. Mr. Dale became a pillar of the miracle for these boxes of food to be sent to so many people in need. This journey has certainly created lasting friendships and visible blessings from God. Looking back at the journey, I can say that it hasn't been easy, especially learning a new language, but I consider that it has been paved with solid footings and security for my wife and kids. When I see people around us and, on the news, coming to this country with really nothing, I consider that we are all blessed each day in this great country.

(Jose' received the Teacher of the Year from his school in 2020.)

Deniana

I worked in the internal Audit department of a company in Venezuela while my husband worked as an operator of manufacturing. However, our lives were in danger because the government persecuted us for disagreeing with their policies. When we moved to America, the first year was very difficult. Financially, we wondered if we would ever make it in this new world. Sometimes, we wanted to leave and be reunited with family we loved back in Venezuela.

Family Hope has been a great fundamental support for our family. People like Rosangela and Gledys have lifted our hopes and been an instrument of God to guide us and provide us the basics of food and love. God has been good to us to send them to us.

My family is very grateful to this beautiful country for the opportunity to start over with our determination and dedication to make a new life in America. We are in the process of becoming economically stable and believe that all things are possible. We have great hope to achieve our objectives on the path of success in America. We know God will provide us with a life of health and happiness along with our hard work and determination to give back to this great country.

Wilmar

I was a professor of Civil Engineering and owned a family business of stores for children's clothes. I was active in the Democratic Political Party, which was in opposition to the government regime. One night when I was driving to one of the stores, I was attacked while my wife and daughter were with me. They hit me on the head, and I fell down unconscious. My wife started screaming. A person from across the street came to our side. But when I woke up, my aggressor was holding my wife. He hit me again, and I fell to the ground. Finally, people began coming toward us and the aggressor fled. The aggressor was identified by witnesses as a relative connected with the government.

Almost immediately I could feel that my left side was paralyzed and even right side except my right hand. So, I was referred to a specialist and discovered that I had inflammation of the brain and had to have surgery. I was transported to a larger hospital for surgery. It took one year to recover from the operation. I was in the hospital for six months. Also, my wife was hurt with five fractures in the foot. For two years, I pursued the aggressor, making reports to the police. I would remember the words of the aggressor, "Whenever I see you, I will kill you."

It took me two years until I concluded that I needed to leave Venezuela. During that time, I continued to be pursued and threatened by criminals sent by the government. They killed our dog. They broke things around our house.

In 2020, I had flight tickets out of the country, but due to the pandemic, all the borders were closed so I continued to be terrorized. Finally, in March 2021, the airport was open, and I was able to leave Venezuela.

I landed in Miami and was offered a hotel room by a friend. I left everything behind...all my stores and inventory. All material things were left behind. Then I booked a ticket to Houston where my brother lives. I was so happy to stay a month. I showed him the scars on my head.

I am not the kind of person to just sit around so I began looking for a job. I was told about Family Hope Food Fairs and heard about

Gledys. This became a big help in my transition while I was finding jobs cleaning pools and any other jobs that I could find. Finally, I became a Project Manager for building a bridge and pipeline, something I had already experience with in Venezuela. On the weekends, I would volunteer at Family Hope to give back to the Venezuelans who were struggling even more.

Now after all those years, my wife and children are managers of a fast-food franchise. We have all the necessary legal documents. I feel gratitude for the people of America! I have encountered so many wonderful people willing to help, lend support in the hardest and uncertain times. When we left Venezuela, we didn't have a plan but just ran for our lives.

America has given me a home! I have felt the warmth of friendship and constant support. Still today, I will not forget Gledys at Family Hope in sharing with me groceries and genuine care.

When I look back, this was the right decision guided by God to leave Venezuela. Contrary to what people might say that you will be rejected if you speak Spanish, I have only experienced acceptance and love from Americans. I have no second thoughts. I will continue to walk by the hands of God. My children have a bright future. In this country, they can do whatever they dream. They are in music, sports, ballet. My oldest son just graduated from high school and wants to major in Mechanical Engineering. Americans, thank you for a new life! You are truly a land of opportunities.

Luz

I worked for 16 years in a worldwide corporation. I was the head of the supply chain and managed three shipping ports, production, procurement and planning. I am a CPA with an MBA in Finance.

By 2016, the military was watching the neighborhoods and taking note of our activities. One day, I came out of a building, and someone smashed my head against the stone wall and showed me a picture of my son. Now this picture wasn't any picture of my son. I had to be taken inside the private school that he attended. This scared me. I had heard so many stories of medical professionals being persecuted. As a result, I told my mother that I was moving to the U.S.

I had a very dear friend, and she was called to the Police station. She was raped and put in prison for no reason. As I saw what happened to my friend, I was determined to start a new life in America. Therefore, I sold all my things and came to the U.S. with two suitcases. Later, I was told that the police were contacting neighbors to find where I was. With tears in my eyes, I had to tell my son when we reached America that we were not going back. His response was: "Mommy, you lied to me. You told me we were going on a holiday." I had no choice if I wanted my family safe.

It broke my heart to hear my son cry for the first month. I would ask myself, "Would he ever get over this hurt?" His father gave me full custody which was best for my son. Now I was beginning a new life in the U.S., divorced with a son to raise by myself. In the beginning, my son would ask, "Mommy, are we poor?" I would remind him, "Son, we are rich in education, rich in opportunities, rich in freedom." I told him that you can't negotiate freedom. You don't need to bend your knees to someone just to please others. This is a free land with many opportunities.

I remember sitting in a circle and playing a game with co-workers. Everyone was to say one thing nice about the person to your right. My son said about me, "My mom is a dream chaser." We talked about how we can live in America and not be harmed, continuously learn, and respect others.

Some of my new neighbors in America would ask, "How do you know so much?" I shared how I went to school, researched, networked to refine my purpose God has given me. I cried so much, but I would not look back. I discovered that in my praying, I would be confirmed as a leader. On my darkest day, people would contact me. On my darkest day, I could be a light to others. I found my purpose by helping others.

Without a doubt, this is the greatest country in the world…a land of opportunities. With the right decisions you make, you will have a garden flourishing. For me, Katy, TX has been a warm community that has welcomed me. Now I lead a team of twenty engineers with amazing diversity who respect me. I believe my focus is a responsibility to make the right decisions. I have a son who is diabetic. In this country, he has all the help he needs. Each of us are placed in our neighborhood and community with a gift to take the necessary risks, be responsible, give back to others, and make decisions with no regrets. It is like the Parable of the Talents. All were given gifts. Each of us can decide to grow and help others.

Americans should never take for granted this land of freedom. Communism in Venezuela only wants one thing: CONTROL. The government wants to control our lives, so the elite have all the power with less dignity for the people. In America, our government is FOR THE PEOPLE. No other country is built on that premise. Thank you, America, for this beautiful land of opportunity!

Letti

I am Venezuelan and had three children before my husband died. I was determined to provide a good life for my children. I graduated with an education degree and taught Elementary and Junior High School for 25 years. I am also a criminal lawyer and worked as a Legal Associate.

Before our government was in decline, one of my children came to live in the U.S.A. through a sponsor. I came to visit my son in America. I fell in love with the city where he lived. It was not in my plans to live in America, but God had plans for safety. My middle son was kidnapped while living in Venezuela, and these criminals tried to extort money from him. This was a very terrifying season. My youngest daughter also decided to come to live in this beautiful country. Finally, I was happy because all of us were together and safe.

I remember the first months here in America were difficult, particularly the customs and language. I felt isolated because I did not see many neighbors nor communicate with them. I felt so shy about not speaking very good English. At first, I was dependent on my children. They were busy with their work, so I was alone most of the day. All that monies that I had worked for retirement in Venezuela no longer existed. I remember feeling so sad that I was living in a country and neighborhood where I could barely speak English, and I depended on my children for basic living. I felt so alone!

My greatest joy was when my son bought his first house and car. I began to drive and look for churches which spoke Spanish. In time, I met people at the Church of Christ Church, and began to learn a few words of English with many new friendships. One of those friends was Gledys from Family Hope. She encouraged me to enroll in English classes and be a volunteer at Family Hope's

Food Fair and Back-to-School shoes program. I also met a super special person, a man with a heart of gold and filled with kindness, Mr. Dale, an angel.

Today, I have a special friendship with Gledys and so many friends. I have dedicated myself in helping whoever I can. I collect objects and help furnish apartments for those who were like me a few years ago. So many Venezuelan families come with nothing. Some do not even have the money to buy a car. I do my part to help them furnish their apartments and make a better life in America. Thanks be to God that I am 78 years old, and I still feel very good as I help others. It is great to be alive!

Rafael

My name is Rafael. I was in one of the first groups to arrive in the U.S. from Venezuela. In 2003, my wife and two children decided to live in the U.S. We came looking for freedom where all the rules and laws were applied equally. At that time, we believed that freedom and liberty were worth the risk of leaving Venezuela to come to this new land of opportunity. Since we had vacationed in America before, the U.S. was not new to us, but this time was different as we planned to live in America for the rest of our lives.

I still remember the day, December 23, 2002, I was working at the oil company. The Venezuela government was increasingly wanting to control more of the oil companies' business. On this day in history, a group of armed "Chavez Army" showed up at our work site and said, "Now we take control!" They replaced the manager with a new manager, and they fired all of us. We were not allowed to go up to the office to Human Resources. For the next few days, I visited other oil companies for a possible job, and all had a sign telling us not to apply. As a result, no other oil company would hire us as demanded by the government. We were labelled, "Petro Terrorists!" As a result, it was an easy decision to leave Venezuela. There was a saying among the workers, "This is Saturday for every pig. Today a pig. Tomorrow the rest of the people." (Meaning, the ruthless government eventually comes for all the people.) I sat with my wife, and said, "Let's move. We need to try a new life!"

Why did we choose the United States? Simply, we did not trust any of the Latin countries. Though the four countries of Ecuador, Columbia, Peru and Bolivia were known as "Our Brothers," they did not have stable economies. As a result, we flew to Tampa, FL and stayed for two and a half months with family. In 2003, we received the necessary documents. In 2004, My sister was killed, and we would be tested if we could trust the American judicial system. It seemed it took so long for the man to be brought to justice. In fact, in my anger, I said to the detective, "In Venezuela, money is passed under the table to let people like him go free. Is this what is happening here?" He assured me not. Months went on, and finally there was a trial for this man who murdered my sister. I was so relieved when I heard the words from the jury, "Guilty!" Later, the detective, who I shared my frustration, whispered to me, "Rafael, I told you." The American system had worked.

I view America as a great land of opportunities. In 2007, I received a job as an Engineer. I cried out to God, "Thank you, God, there is a purpose for me." I promised I would not complain about my job. I think back at all the other jobs I had like Wendy's, which helped me learn English. I learned: "Be honest and go the extra mile."

America is a beautiful country with a variety of landscapes like Boston, Miami, Texas, San Diego, Seattle and the Great Plains.

For Venezuelans, the attraction to the U.S. is the safe neighborhoods. All Venezuelans want to live in a place where we are not threatened by the government.

I have strong feelings regarding the Border crossings. If a family said to me that they were going to cross the Border today, I would say, "You're crazy!" Yes, America is a land of opportunities, but the risk is so high in crossing the Border, I could not suggest it for anyone. My suggestion about the Border is that we are strict with the laws and do not open the Border for good and bad people to come. Do not just release those who come over the Border but have a system in place to take care of them as Americans. It is not fair to those of us who came legally, and those who are still awaiting citizenship to allow these people to just walk across the Border. We came legally to America and expect others to do the same. It is disrespectful to cross the Border illegally just because you want a better life. America is a land of rules, and all should respect these laws, including our politicians. We are grateful to be part of America!

Yianfranco

I was a worker in a thermoelectric plant in Venezuela. Throughout the years, I was in many situations that tested my integrity and would impact my family. In my job, there were times that people of authority broke rules and treated other workers so badly. I still have memories of my friends being sentenced to jail for nothing or even being killed. Government officials had so much control over our lives.

Now we are in our first few months of life in the new world of America. We came with nothing but our faith in God and belief that in America everything is possible. My faith in God and the future of my son keeps me going every day. The greatest joy is to feel safe without being worried that something bad will happen to us at any time. My second greatest joy is the best education that my son will receive.

The most difficult is the language barrier. There are days we feel very frustrated in not speaking English better, but we are improving. We know that speaking English is our doorway to better jobs. We are so grateful to live in America filled with opportunities!

Gaby

I graduated with a law degree in Venezuela and was a professor of law at the university. However, one year on my birthday at about 9pm, five armed men entered my house and took my two-year old daughter, my three-year-old niece and my sisters, and brother-in-law and myself and locked all of us in a room for 30 minutes, threatening us with death, targeting the babies first. They said they would return to deal with us again. As a result, we decided to leave our country immediately and fled to Chile. After several years in Chile, we began to see the country's economic, political, and social situations were becoming complicated and filled with the increase of crime and xenophobia. Finally, we made the decision to come to the United States, using our American visa relying on uncles and cousins in America to help us.

I believe that we fortunate to have family already in the U.S. But the mind tries to play tricks on you and your emotions get out of control, so you question everything. Was this the right decision?

It has been a slow immigration process. We have had some medical situations, and it has become challenging to pay for any health treatments, so we try to stay healthy. Certainly, the language barrier has caused us a delay in good-paying jobs and advancement opportunities. But we are studying hard to be proficient in English. Another concern is the health of our parents in Venezuela. We took the risk to leave Venezuela for a better life and yet we become very sad when we remember our parents who struggle with their health as they grow older in Venezuela. We miss them!

My greatest refuge is God who did not abandon us and placed good people in our paths at just the right time. We treasure our extended family in America. What a joy! Two of the angels sent by God included Rosangela and Gledys from Family Hope. They have given us so many services with food and assistance that we never thought possible. We are grateful for them.

Rosairys

I am from Venezuela and have a degree in education. I had a beautiful and happy life in our country until I had to leave because the politicians were so bad and threatening to us. We came to America with almost nothing except a suitcase of dreams filled with hope and faith in God to guide me.

Almost immediately, I was introduced to Family Hope who supported me with food and furniture. They were there to give me advice, but most of all, their joy and encouragement gave me the confidence to succeed in this new country. I have discovered this is a great country with generous people waiting to help. Now we are on a path to start over with our lives and contribute back to this nation. In honesty, it has not been easy to adapt to a new country, a new city, and new ways of living, but I am surrounded by wonderful people who have supported me and guided me. I thank God for leading me to this day.

Annie

I came to the United States just a month ago. It feels so good to be here after living in Ecuador for 6 years. We left Venezuela for Ecuador because our lives were threatened. My husband had a successful job in Venezuela, managing commercial buildings for 13 years. One day he was approached by two men to interview for a government job. He declined the offer. Later, two gentlemen broke into a car by his commercial buildings. The next day, a man came and explained that the car belonged to a government official and $40,000 was taken from the car. My husband was threatened by this man, "Look at the video and tell us who the burglar is by tomorrow or we will kill you and your family." My husband began to look at the video and ask the neighbors. They told him, "He is part of the organization working for the president to hack internet information." With the threat of harm to particularly my husband, we set a plan to leave Venezuela. In the 26 years that I have known my husband, I have never seen his face so filled with fear. For the past few years, we have seen an increase in crime. With two children, we desired a safe place to raise our children. And this is our hope for children in the U.S.: They will have good education and a safe place to live.

Now after a month in America, we are grateful for the people of Ecuador who welcomed us. However, because so many Venezuelans are fleeing to Ecuador, we are often rejected.

America has been wonderful to accept us. We are so happy to be here in America.

When I look back, I see that Venezuelans made poor decisions in our voting for the wrong people to lead our government. Everything sounded good when they campaigned, but their policies and choices of government officials led to the destruction of our beautiful country.

We are grateful to God for allowing us to finally come to America. Already, we have met some very generous people like Gledys at Family Hope. I know it won't be easy, but we will make it by God's grace. This is a good country...a safe place with good education for our children. I know we have a good future!

Andreas

We are born with the principle of defending freedom. It is the basis of humanity and brings dignity to the citizens. In Venezuela, I viewed the government that came into power as "everything for themselves." Their main goal was to have the people to "depend on them" so they could control you while the elite get everything. It didn't happen overnight, but slowly the Venezuelan people were forced to their knees.

For example, I witnessed an evolution in the country. The government had enough money, so they gave almost everyone a car. If you were married, they might give you a house. As the government was flooding the economy with things, inflation began to rise, and people were becoming controlled and losing their freedom. Someone may ask, "How can people exist on

$30/month? Answer: They don't need money for a house, gas, or food. However, eventually, the government took all the freebies away. They now had the people dependent on them. The people were controlled. Now 70%-80% of Venezuelans work for the government. It is like a frog in the kettle that gradually gets boiled. It is slow but certain death for people's freedom.

My advice to Americans is: Take great pride in your beautiful country. Love your country. People will try and make America look bad by saying, "You are bad because of racism." Hate that tactic! Continue to love your country. People make this country great. I don't see any other country that was built on "For the People." All other governments expect the people to serve the elite and government regime. Be in love with America! I am so grateful to live in America with such generous people!

Dianiret

In 2016, I decided to leave Venezuela, my home country. Why? I wanted a better life for my family, and I did not want to be threatened by the police anymore.

I owned a boutique close to the government offices. My husband had a business next to mine. Sometimes people would protest in the street against the government. My husband would sometimes record these protests. When government officials found out that he had recorded some of the protests, they threatened him and broke his nose. The government wanted those videos, but my husband would not give them to these corrupt officials. The organization that is like the IRS came to my business to ask for more taxes if I was to keep my business open. By December of 2021, I closed all the stores after being threatened with my life.

After hiding in our apartment, we stayed four more months before we made the big risk to come to the U.S. Through all this, we shared a sadness that members of our family had died of COVID. We had only been in the U.S. a short time when we heard that my brother and father had died.

We were fortunate that my husband's cousin allowed us to stay in his garage for a month. Since that time, life has been better. We are no longer in danger from the police. Americans have welcomed us, and we have experienced lots of opportunities.

We are so grateful for Family Hope. We had only been in America five days when we were contacted by Gledys of Family Hope. She has truly become a friend and has helped us with so many resources and needs. Family Hope has given us food at the food fairs and has lovingly delivered pillows, towels and beds to our apartment.

I want everyone to know how blessed this country is. None of us make it by ourselves. There are so many good people to help and support us along the way. We are so grateful to God who has worked through the caring faces of Family Hope. We don't take it for granted that we are now safe. We can go to work and go to school, and we feel safe. Amazing! Thanks to all of you for helping us make a better life!

REFLECTIONS: Fleeing from...Running to

I believe the Roman Empire and Venezuela have something in common in the way they treated their people. Today, if you go to Israel, the most beloved image seen on mosaics, in windows, in church floors and painted on plates in the marketplace is the "fish and loaves." Why is this miracle story so treasured? I believe it is both on the miracle side of life and a political story. When Jesus fed the 5,000 people (probably 10,000 – 15,000 people counting women and children) and asked them to sit down, he took five loaves and two fish and provided food for all present and even leftovers. Amazement overcame the disciples and the people gathered to witness this miracle! However, during that time, miracles also received opposition because the bread became a political statement. Caesar Augustus, Emperor of Rome, had promised to be the provider for the people by giving the people a loaf of bread regularly. However, during this time of the miracle, Rome had negated this promise. They were not giving bread to the families on a regular basis. After the miracle of "Feeding of the 5,000," Jesus was seen as the one who provided bread to the people in contrast to Tiberius Caesar Augustus, sometimes called, "Son of God" and "Lord," who betrayed his promise of being the provider. Jesus was the faithful Son of God while Rome betrayed the trust of the people. Jesus lived up to his promise of being the "Bread of Life."

In many of the Venezuelan stories, you heard the cries against the present government as the leaders betrayed the trust of the people. What began with a new revolution in the late 90's to provide for the people has now been corrupted by political killings, unjust imprisonments, ruthless actions by the military and police, and now a broken economy where inflation causes many to use the Black-market to buy the very basics of bread, water and medicine. What was once a thriving beautiful nation has now turned into a harsh and poverty-stricken life.

For many, life changed quickly in fleeing from the corrupt government of Venezuela and running to freedom in America. When Venezuelans arrived in America, they spoke about fleeing from the ruthless dictatorship and communism that turned a prosperous nation, which reaped the benefits of oil, to majoring in drug trafficking and starving their people.

The question in everyone's mind is: What are the Venezuelans running to? In the stories, you will read the dreams repeated: 1) Freedom...to be free to work and lead a life filled with purpose and without controls from the government. 2) Liberty...to be treated fairly by the government, police, and judicial system. 3) Safety...so parents can send their child out to play without the fear of the child being abducted and held for ransom. 4) A bright new future for their children so they have all the options of good schools and jobs to live the very best life.

Simon Bolivar was known for freeing the five Latin countries of Peru, Ecuador, Columbia, Venezuela and Bolivia. In the past, Venezuelans called these other four countries "their brothers." Today, these four countries have economic and political challenges of their own, and they worry about Venezuelans with good education arriving to their country and taking their jobs. As a result, the Venezuelans turned to the United States, where they had previously vacationed, as a haven where they could make their home. They have been impressed by the Hollywood media and the variety of beautiful scenic landscapes in America. They view America as a safe place where everyone abides by a set of rules and lives honestly...something they did not have in Venezuela. They even mention the ease of our transportation where everyone abides by the rules to avoid chaos and congestion.

Venezuelans have experienced triple digit inflation because of their government's leadership. Repeatedly, they warn Americans of the cruel effects of inflation. After hearing many cries for help and listening to stories of trying to stretch the family budget to afford enough protein rich food (i.e. meat) and nutritious food to feed the family, I want to wave a red flag about INFLATION, and its demeaning effect on those already struggling month to month, which includes Venezuelans. There are no photos of people marching and protesting in the streets because of inflation, either in Venezuela or America. It is a sly tax by politicians that hits the most fragile families. Politicians like to use the poor to justify their ways, but seldom benefit the poor. For example, Venezuelans recall when Venezuela shifted from majoring in oil production to drug trafficking, the jobs and flow of money changed directions from the working people to the elite of the country who are the military and government officials. Thus, the poor suffered even more.

Likewise in America, the rate of inflation has increased. As a result, the website of cnbc.com reports 64% of Americans are now living paycheck to paycheck, and as of May 12, 2022, Americans are paying an extra $341 per month because of the increase inflation costs of groceries, clothes, housing, and other basic goods. Most middle-class families and wealthier in America will find ways to pay the extra $341/month costs perhaps from savings or the use of credit cards. However, many of the families I served were severely impacted by the $341/month increase in costs from inflation and had to make severe life-changing choices with their living expenses. Some bought less meat for their family. Most often, I was contacted for assistance for rent. The extra $341 in costs now reduces the $2,000 per month of income to $1659, which is the average cost of rent for an apartment in the area. Then, what happens during a pregnancy when the mother needs to stay home or is a single mom? What does the family live on after paying the rent? This is where Family Hope and other non-profits are contacted to provide rental assistance, so the family is not evicted, and children are not uprooted from their schools. Yet, no one is protesting in the streets over inflation. In fact, some elites in our society gloat because it will be better for everyone. When are families better off when they scramble to have enough food? Everyone deserves to eat! Venezuelans would agree that Americans need to keep our politicians accountable! Do your own research on the causes of inflation. The ones who consider themselves elite will not be affected by inflation, but the lowest of incomes and fixed incomes will be crushed. The best ways to help those economically challenged are wise money management and wise politicians to keep a low inflation rate. Do not accept the myth that the poor will benefit by larger spending. I have seen first-hand the suffering of our brothers and sisters in need because of inflation.

Venezuelans grieve the broken promises and wide-spread poverty today. As you read the Venezuelan stories and listen to them, you hear them describe the beautiful memories of their past homeland and sadness of their country evolving into Communism. From their conversations, here is a summary from the Venezuelans writings and conversations of a once prosperous nation turned into poverty and less freedom:

First, the Venezuelans remember the days prior to the new Regime with small Ma and Pa shops, entrepreneurs, and businesses thriving with close relationships with employees and customers. They excelled in hard work and had many friendships. The government had minimal controls and did not threaten them with violence. Their life in the workplace flourished.

Second, when the new regime came to power, leaders embraced a new attraction to expansive government and more controls. At first, many citizens were given cars and expensive gifts to win over the people's support. Quickly, this generosity was replaced with threats to join Government-run systems, using ruthless tactics or even imprisonment to persuade allegiance. The new model was,

"The Collective System," which was more important than the individual. Personal dignity and Human Rights were considered less important. More rules were created to protect and preserve the expanding government, resulting in less freedom. Gradually, the Government System had a hunger for more taxes to satisfy the cost of a larger system. The narrative became, "More taxes will help the poor and everyone." Consequently, inflation skyrocketed.

Third, the leadership used corrupt ways to govern. They allowed for only one voice and squashed all opposing ideas. Many look back and admit the mistake of voting Marxist leaders into office. Harsh controls eliminated their freedom once experienced. The new model was: Use any means necessary to restrict the opposition, using punishment, if necessary, to breed fear in the people.

Finally, the result today is a government who betrayed the trust of the people. What began as a promise of equity for all the people evolved into hurting the poor and bringing poverty and hardship to the whole nation.

To summarize, in my conversations with the Venezuelans, these are THEIR words to Americans to preserve basic principles of governing and electing leaders:
1. Don't let your leaders mislead you. They are your servants. You are the only country in the world that states "by the people." No matter what party affiliation you are...Democrat, Republican, Independent, make your politicians serve you and be accountable. We now lament, "We believed in the newly elected leaders' promises, but they betrayed our trust."
2. Do not make excuses for your government leaders when they make decisions that are unfair or bend the rules. Insist the laws apply fairly to all, unlike that of Venezuela where

military and political leaders have a different set of rules than the people.

3. Be careful of the slippery slope. What started out as a promise for free things for the people has turned into a country of a Black-market economy. Remember nothing is free! Someone always pays.

4. Do not let inflation destroy your economy. It hurts both the lower incomes and the seniors the most who cannot afford the price increases. As a result, the whole nation struggles. Today, the shelves in Venezuela lack basic needs of food and medicine.

5. Be careful how you vote. Do your research on the candidates for office. Know their past and their reasons to serve. You have a beautiful country admired by many around the world. Do not allow your nation to be led by politicians who twist the truth and allow the country to bend the rules to their advantage.

6. Be careful of government-created "elitism." Venezuelans have been told repeatedly by leaders with less education than they, "We know better than you." Political leaders and their followers will try to persuade you to create an elite club, controlling the opinions of all. In America, beware of those who tell you, "We know better than you about this idea so just follow us." Remember, America was built on the vision for everyone to be given opportunities and freedom to pursue their dreams.

7. Do not allow foreign governments to take advantage of your natural resources and economy. Venezuela is now being controlled by powers and monetary advantage of Russia, China, and Cuba. Be careful about how you allow foreign powers to control your economy or political leadership.

8. We love America. We hear many Americans who are disappointed in America or even hate America. Every country has part of their history they either regret or wish

they could wipe out of the textbooks. Venezuelans just escaped from a ruthless and corrupt government and are now running to this country to live a new life of opportunities. We still believe in America! Continue to right the past wrongs and improve America. Especially, know that as Venezuelans, we will choose to live in safe neighborhoods with excellent schools. We have experienced immeasurable violence and never want to fear for our lives again or for our families' lives. As a result, you will see us settle in places away from high crime. We are willing to sacrifice for a safe community. What you have in America is a beautiful country and a unique system "for the people" and expect your leaders to be your servants. Venezuela has never experienced that. We are grateful to live in America, and someday hope to share in the privilege of being American citizens.

QUESTIONS:

1. How can you share your convictions and listen respectfully to those who have a differing opinion or experience?
2. Discuss each of the eight warnings articulated by the Venezuelans.
3. What is your passion to help those struggling economically in America?
4. What can you learn from the Venezuelan?

CHAPTER THREE

DNA Kindness & Work

Maria L.

I worked as a Trade Marketing Manager for a Tobacco company in Venezuela. I oversaw 14 marketing representatives across the country and did extensive travel. I engaged with new clients, developed current clients and promoted the sales of our top products. As I saw the diminishing lifestyle in our country, I made the difficult choice to leave Venezuela. My biggest reason to leave now was for my daughter's future. I saw a very bleak existence in the years to come.

To make things even more difficult, my daughter was extremely emotional about leaving the rest of our family behind since we were a very close family with parents and grandparents. COVID hit right after we arrived in America, and the U.S. immigration agency closed nationwide, leaving us with no answers about our immigration process. At first it was so hard because I didn't have a work permit, but thankfully Family Hope was there to greet us within the first two weeks. They gave us food and so much help and encouragement. I will never forget those first few weeks.

I believe it was God who sent Mr. Dale and Family Hope into our lives. They are truly family to me. On the night of December 2019, just a few weeks after my daughter and I moved to Katy, we received a last-minute invitation to a Christmas concert sponsored by a local church, Second Baptist Church. I remember boarding the bus in front of Walmart filled with parents and children to be brought to this church. That night, I met two of the most supportive and caring people on this earth, Gledys and Rosangela from Family Hope. Then Gledys introduced me to Mr. Dale and his very welcoming spirit. He asked me about my English because I guess I had very good pronunciation. So, I explained about my previous experience as an ESL teacher back in Venezuela. In our discussion, it felt like we were heroes for that night. I remember getting off the bus in front of the church and a large line of people were waiting to welcome us. They were clapping and greeting us as we entered. They provided us with food and snacks. The last presentation was a choir of kids who sang Christmas jingles. The whole auditorium sang with them as one big family. It was beautiful and beyond what I would have expected on that very first Christmas in the U.S. After the event was over, we left the church and boarded the bus, only to find toys for each kid and one gift card for every adult on that bus. My daughter received a beautiful doll and after almost three years, she still has it. Every time I see that doll it reminds me of that night when I felt as if we were home. I was and still am thankful to God for letting me live and feel that moment. It was as if God was telling me, "You're in the right place." That night our story began, and it's been one blessing after another. I knew I was living in a neighborhood of very generous hearts! This event changed our lives!

Once again, my life has changed 180 degrees when I met the man who would become my husband and father to my son. He is also the best father to my seven-year-old daughter who is now a second grader. He speaks fluently in English and Spanish. I have a wonderful family and a great career that has now become my passion and purpose in life.

In the following months, I discovered hope beyond all expectations. My daughter and I started a new life from zero. From Family Hope, I received so much help, and I volunteered at Family Hope Food Fairs to give back for all they had done for us.

I personally think America is a cultural melting pot, and I have met so many who wish the best for us. I feel blessed to have a wonderful job that can support my family. I now serve as a Spanish Translator for a popular Parent class sponsored by Family Hope. These parent classes have helped hundreds of families who recently moved to the U.S. by focusing on the children and what they go through in school as new immigrants. Life is Good in America!

Andrea

Like many Venezuelans, I left our country in search of a better future for our children. The crisis in our country had already knocked on our door in many ways, including lack of security, monetary decline, and quality of food. It was very easy and fast to eat the "savings" covering basic needs even with good jobs. In a few months, I gave birth to my second child. When I was pregnant, we would spend more than 20 days without electricity in the city where we lived. So, we had enough, and decided to immigrate to the U.S. since we could not wait for nine months of pregnancy to know if I would have a safe delivery or have complications. We wanted to be sure to preserve the life of our son.

Arriving in a country where the language and culture are totally different made life difficult at first. Also, we had never experienced the reality that working one job for 8-10 hours per day would not be enough income to live. All the physical effort and psychological adapting could not give us enough funds to make it in this new country. Soon we had to ask for help in the churches, something we never had to do before. With the greatest humility in our hearts, knowing it would be temporary, we asked many churches, and they graciously extended a generous hand giving us food and spiritual help.

God has blessed us in a very special way by putting Family Hope and their team in our path. They unselfishly watched over us and cared for our well-being. On several occasions, they saved my family. I don't know what would become of us if they hadn't opened the doors to faith and hope for us. There have been hard times and a lot of work, many sacrifices, but we know that God has accompanied us through every day of our life in the U.S. As a result, we can "give back" what we have received at every opportunity.

In closing, thanks to the whole team of Family Hope that make things possible for many of us, so we do not lose hope. Mr. Hope, you have been our inspiration! You helped our marriage when we thought that everything was lost because we did not have enough money or food to feed our children. You found me a wonderful job that I will be forever grateful. My mother passed away and that caused me to go into a deep depression to add to our difficulties. The whole team was there for us, holding out their friendly hands. The Holidays in December are the most important for Venezuelans since they are times to share together in family reunions. In this new country, we discovered the beautiful moments of family and never being alone. Thanks for the opportunity to live in this generous country.

Jorge

I am a mechanical engineer, turbomachinery specialist. I worked for more than 25 years in the oil and gas industry in Venezuela. In January 2019, while I was in the United States, I was informed that I had to go back to Venezuela. My wife and I evaluated the situation in Venezuela. Thinking about the future for our children, we decided to stay in the U.S. and look for new opportunities in this country. After some months, our savings were depleted, and we went through a difficult time. We did not have enough money to buy food and pay rent. God listened to our prayers, and someone told us about an organization called Family Hope that help families with food. In October 2019, for the first time in our life, we were in a line of cars waiting for food to feed our family. My wife was out of the car, and someone approached her. She did not speak English, but that person was kind and full of love. Mr. Dale gave us a gift card which we used for additional food. We received more blessings and help to prepare for a Thanksgiving dinner when Family Hope gave us assistance to pay our rent for two months.

We believe God puts the right people in our path in time of need to help us. Mr. Dale is one of those people. Today, we are getting better, but we will always be grateful for the help given to us by Family Hope during our hardest time. We still volunteer at Family Hope and try to help people who are going through the same situation. I encourage you to volunteer at a place like Family Hope and show people they are not alone. There is always hope. God loves them. Find out what these beautiful organizations need. People in need appreciate your sincere help. Our thanks for Family Hope!

Julette

Venezuela was already dangerous, but it got much worse around 2014, so my parents decided we needed to leave for our safety. As a teenager, I came to the U.S. several months before my parents arrived in 2014, and I stayed with a family member I did not know. It was very hard for me as I'm very close to my family. I felt lost and lonely. Even though I was in a better place for my future, I was sad most of the time. I missed my family so much.

Back in Venezuela we used to have large family gatherings every week, but now we could only talk over the phone. I'm glad that we have the tools to text and even videocall, but it's not the same as being present. At the beginning I had no friends. Making friends has never been easy for me. The last year I spent in Venezuela I was starting to open up to other people, but then I moved, and because of my insecurities, fears and language barrier, I closed myself again from others. I remember crying every day in math class because I did not understand, and I just wanted to go home where my family was. I felt that I was falling behind with everything. I couldn't catch up with the people who had been born here. It was difficult for me to adapt to this change.

For a long time, I was just hoping it would be temporary. I wanted everything to be fixed or to at least improve enough so I could go back to Venezuela with my friends and family. I wanted my stay in the US to be no more than just a short learning experience. I could not see myself here.

I came here at an age that was perfect for me to take advantage of academic opportunities, this also should have made it easier for me to adapt to this area in general; however, this was also a time in which I started to struggle with insecurities of my own. On a personal level, I was struggling with my self-image and the constant feeling that I was falling behind. Self-esteem shifts and emotions that are a normal part of growing up were mixed with all the changes and grief that come with leaving my culture, home, and family. I was always dreaming about seeing my loved ones again.

I saw from a distance how everyone in the family was going their separate ways, some having to stay in Venezuela, others having to leave to other countries in Latin America. Everyone going through their own struggles of either suffering because of the country's corruption or facing the challenges of immigrating to other countries in which Venezuelans were not warmly welcomed.

This brings a sadness I cannot really explain. I just wish it didn't have to be like this, but part of the issue was that I only focused on the sadness. The feeling of not being where we should be and the uncertainty of whether we would be able to succeed here or have to go back. The situation back in Venezuela was getting worse to the point that going back was not an option. Seeing family members struggle to find food and proper care was heartbreaking, and sometimes we were unable to reach them because of the constant power outages. We needed to focus on finding solutions and taking the opportunities that God has given us to move forward and help our family. After some time, I was able to slowly adapt. I am fortunate to now live in a safe and culturally diverse area.

Every life change comes with its challenges. Dealing with constant uncertainty, not being as financially stable as we were back in our country, having to adapt and learn a new language, learning everyday about how daily life aspects are handled here… It's part of life. I now know that everyone has a different life experience, and everyone goes through life at their own pace. Learning from others and how distinct everyone's life journey is one of the things that makes life so beautiful.

My outlook has changed, thanks to the support of others, mostly from my mom. She is my inspiration. My mom is the most amazing person, and the one I love the most in the whole world. She has been through so much, but her sweetness and light keep shining bright, even brighter than before. One of the reasons that I was able to succeed so well in school was because of my mom. From very early in my years, she would read books to me and continually teach me reading and math.

Now, I'm more open and optimistic. My parents and little sister are here. I have been able to meet wonderful people. I am surrounded by love and kindness. I have many opportunities in this country to succeed as an individual and to help my loved ones, as well as people of my community and beyond. I am truly blessed to be here. Many people have helped me and taught me along the way. I have no words to express how blessed and grateful I am.

To this day I'm still unable to visit the rest of my family. I did not know the day I left Venezuela would be the last day I saw a loved one. I am extremely grateful to be in a much safer place with infinite opportunities, but I feel so sad to see how my family back in Venezuela are still struggling because of the country's situation. We must just continue to work hard, sharing as a family as much as possible regardless of the distance, supporting each other and trusting everything in the hands of God.

I thank God for the opportunities and blessings that fill our lives. I want to stay here and keep learning. I want to thank you again for being part of our lives, Dr. Dale. Your love and kindness have lifted so many families including ours. God bless you.

Hugomar   (Interviewed by a friend who knows Hugomar)

My very good friend arrived in the U.S.A. in 2017. Together with his family, they came to America from Venezuela because they were blessed to be selected in the Diversity Visa (Visa Lottery).

I met my friend the day that we moved into our apartment. Coincidentally, they also rented an apartment in the same building. He said that he heard us speaking in Spanish and approached us and asked us what country we were from. I told him Venezuela. He looked astonished because he had also heard my husband speak in Chinese. I could tell that he was very worried living in a new country and not being able to speak English. He did not know the system of how to find a job. We told him not to worry because between our two families, we could figure this out and support each other.

My friend is a Civil Engineer and very religious. He said he has entrusted himself to God to help him and guide him. Because of his faith in God, he can show little fear and approach workers and ask about the opportunity for a job. As a result, the workers treated him kindly and gave him the phone number of the supervisor. They reassured him that all the workers speak Spanish, and he would do well. Since then, my friend interviewed at a company where 70% of the workers are bilingual, and he has worked for more than two years with great certification in his skills.

Through Family Hope, I met his wife on Saturdays at Family Hope's Food Fairs. He said that he has been so blessed by miracle after miracle to make a new living in the U.S.A. He is very grateful for Family Hope in how he sees them serving the community. On Saturdays, you will find him at the center of activity, helping as many people as possible. So many faces in these cars remind him what it was like only a few years ago when his family came with nothing but determination, hard work, and a deep faith in God for a better future.

Today, my friend has completed another step in the American dream. He managed to buy his first house in America. He has a new job which gives him better benefits and he now just completed the process of becoming a Naturalized Citizen of the United States. Despite all the days of wondering if all this was worth it, my friend is no longer afraid that he won't make it. He has experienced what a new life of opportunities can be. He is eager to learn to be the very best worker and citizen of the United States, a country of noble values with endless opportunities for all.

Rhomi

We are a family of Venezuelan musicians migrating first to Columbia and then to the United States. My husband is a Double Bass player, teacher, producer and cultural manager. I am a violinist and musical pedagogue. Both in Venezuela and Columbia, we had a life already fulfilled. However, it was by the Lord's design that we came to America and Texas. From the very first day, Family Hope with Mr. Dale's team of Gledys and Rosangela became true guardian angels for us. They helped us practically equip our entire house.

We are so grateful for the school supplies and Christmas presents for our children. We have been hit hard financially and yet we have been blessed by so much. It is true…God provides! All these people who have helped us deserve heaven. The only thing we can give back to you is with our music. Count on it when you need it!

With one single word, our time in the U.S. has been filled with "kindness." God bless all of you, Americans.

Lisette

I thought it would be easy to leave Venezuela, but it has been more difficult than I ever imagined. My husband and I have two daughters. Eventually, we were all reunited, but the process took years. I came here in 2016 and I did not speak any English. I had never lived in a foreign country where I didn't speak the language nor understand it. Also, because of the ruthless police force in Venezuela, I am still scared when I see the police. However, I knew there was no future for my kids in Venezuela. Some say wages are now $30/month for everyone, even if you are a surgeon or a teacher. More recently, I have heard the number to be only $5/month.

Living in the U.S. has opened so many doors for my family. I love the people of America. So many are willing to help you and show you the rich opportunities. In earlier years, I cried for so many months. Now, I thank God for giving me a chance in this beautiful country. I never believed that one day I would use my chef skills from Venezuela to teach other Spanish-speaking people about cooking in a healthy way. So often, immigrants come to America and are amazed at all the choices of food, some healthy and some not very good for you. As a result, Family Hope asked me to be the chef for a monthly Zoom class called, "Healthy Choices," which allows me to demonstrate and teach ways to choose and prepare healthy foods. I am so pleased with the response for this monthly class and the opportunity to educate my brothers and sisters who are new to America. I love using my chef skills to teach!

As a new resident of America, I urge you to "follow your dreams." It may get tough. Don't let anyone put you down for your dream. Every day say: "I can do it." I live this every day.

Alvaro

My life is dedicated to music. I have been studying music since I was five years old with the Children's Orchestras and Choirs of Venezuela. I learned to play the double bass and played in many orchestras through the years. After 30 years, I became a director of a music academy and belonged to one of the best orchestras in the world. I was fortunate to travel two or three times a year to other countries. However, I could see that our government was causing many problems for the people, and at the same time, my wife was pregnant. We decided to begin a new life in Columbia.

In the six years in Columbia, I became a professor or the Philharmonic Orchestra. I used many of the experiences from Venezuela to form orchestras for youth and train more musicians. Through my initiatives, I was able to bring the knowledge of music to the classroom. Enriching the cultural education of children and young people through music has been my life dream. When a country develops its music culture, we are all better!

We arrived in the U.S., almost two years ago with two children. I continue to share my musical skills and believe that I can contribute to America to bring music alive to children through orchestras and choirs. I believe our story is just beginning to be written in our new world, but certainly music will continue to fill our lives.

Vilchez

We arrived in this country in 2021 with the help of relatives of my husband. We have two children. My husband worked in the oil industry as an Analyst for the purchase and sale of materials. I am a nurse. Also, I have skills in hair styling and in baking.

The separation from our family and friends was very difficult for us including leaving my husband's aging mother in Venezuela since she does not have an American visa. We left all our household belongings in Venezuela in exchange for a better future for our children. Another reason that we decided to come to

America is health treatment for our son since he suffers from heart failure. It was too risky to rely on the Venezuelan medical treatments since the supplies are often in short supply.

The first few months were difficult but provided great hope by family and friends who directed us to Family Hope as well as churches to receive help with rent and food. As we wait for our case of Political Asylum to be approved, God continues to be our source of strength. Along with the family separation, we worry about the timing of our legal status. When will our Political Asylum be approved? On the other hand, I have witnessed a great miracle in this country. Through God and the medicine in this country, my sister has been able to overcome cancer. All of us are so filled with joy and thanksgiving to God for this healing.

Today, our children are safe in this new country, and we are so grateful. Thank you, Family Hope, for helping us make a new home in America.

Angelica

I was a lawyer in Venezuela and my husband was a businessman. In 2019, our country was becoming increasingly worse in its economics. Costs were rising and the inflation was hurting my husband's commercial business. We began to see that the government was intent on controlling every aspect of our lives. The equivalent of the IRS began making threats upon our lives saying, "Shut down your business or give us money."

We began planning to come to the U.S. in 2014 when I was pregnant with our first child. We traveled to the U.S. so he would be an American citizen. In 2016, we did the same with our second child. He was born too in the U.S.

In 2019, when we were visiting Miami, a friend from childhood offered to sponsor us. He was a providence from God. He took us to a lawyer to help us understand the process. When we left to return to Venezuela, he said, "Think about my offer." At the same time, we became Christians. It was a miracle that God sent this person into our lives.

When we arrived back in Venezuela, we started getting serious in preparing to leave Venezuela. I was pregnant and due in December with our third baby. One day we called our friend in Miami and asked, "Are you still willing to sponsor us?" From that conversation, our friend even came to Venezuela to set the plan to leave. It would cost $40,000. Since I was pregnant and wanted the baby to be born in the U.S., we could not wait. We shut down the business completely and sold everything.

In December 2019, our third child, a daughter, was born in the U.S. We spent a few days in Miami, and then we flew to Houston/Katy, TX. We came with two suitcases for five people. A friend opened their home for us for two weeks until we were able to locate an apartment. We had two mattresses to sleep on the floor. We considered ourselves blessed to be in this new country of freedom. Almost immediately, we found Family Hope who helped us. Mr. Hope and Gledys have been angels in our lives. We will never forget all of the support that we have received along the way. Most importantly, we found spiritual hope at a wonderful church, Parkway Fellowship. Not only can we start a new life and jobs, but we have a spiritual home to grow in our faith. So many blessings!

We are so grateful to God to be here in the United States. Only God could orchestrate our journey to keep us safe and give us so many blessings in this new land. I believe that if you keep your faith and believe that God always watches over you, you will discover how good life can be. Certainly, it has been tough in a new country. I took me awhile to learn English. I was a mom of three children who were very busy and growing. I tell others in my shoes, "Work hard. This is a country of many opportunities. Anyone can make it! Trust God!" Now life is better because we received our Green Card six months ago. Both my husband and I have good jobs. We want to give back to this country and be responsible people to show our gratitude.

Ismael

I didn't really understand why we had to move to the U.S. when my parents first told me we were planning on leaving. They kept explaining how things are getting worse, more dangerous. When you are 13 years old, doing great in school and with good friends, everything seems perfect. I guess it was more of an acquiescent acceptance. My parents knew what was best for me, so my siblings and I went along with their requests. We enrolled in private English classes and swapped the TV to English. From then on, we didn't hear Phineas and Ferb with their dubbed Latin-American accent, and instead got used to the foreign English that was spreading throughout the house.

Life carried on. It was clear that we would leave at the end of the school year, so I tried to
enjoy it as much as possible. I hung out with a ton with my friends and even unwisely got a girlfriend two months before I had to move to the U.S. I thought moving here would be more like an extended vacation. My parents told me that it would be one or two years until things got better, and then we could come back. The reality that it would be a permanent travel did not sink in until much, much later.

We had a plethora of good-bye parties. All the holidays felt bigger than ever. We visited our relatives more frequently and spent more time at their house. There was now an uneasy feeling knowing that those events might have been the last time I would ever see again the friends and family I left behind.

My father had to move to the U.S. about a month before the rest of us. I wish I had been more aware of the things I could have done to help. My mother had to deal with the unsurmountable task of choosing the things to leave behind since we only had so much space in the baggage. We did what here would be called garage sales, except that we lived in an apartment so people would walk into our home to buy our things. Instead of helping, I was distracted and probably made it harder on my mother by constantly asking to go out and see my girlfriend.

The day we flew was a quiet one. It was my mother, sister, brother, and me riding in a taxi at dawn in complete silence. We had flown a lot of times so the experience of being at the airport and riding a plane was not novel to us. What was surprising upon arriving was the wave of heat that greeted us as soon as we arrived in Houston. What was even more unexpected was where we would be living. In cartoons and media, Texas was always pictured as a land full of cowboys, so I thought we were moving to a ranch, riding horses, even possible raising cattle…who knows! Instead, we moved to the quintessential American suburbia, where every house is a carbon copy of each other, the lakes are man-made, and the grass must be bright green year-round.

Luckily my mother had a cousin where we would stay for the first month or two while my parents looked for a house to start paying mortgage on. There was a play station 4 in that house, and I spent way too much time playing there before the school year started. I feel like I owe an apology to my cousin for hogging his ps4 like I did. Looking back, it is clear to see that it was a coping mechanism to distract me from what was happening. Trying to keep long distance relationships as a 14-year-old feels like a cruel joke. I had a phone, so I texted and called my friends and my girlfriend a lot at first. Overtime there are less and less things to text about, and things just kind of died off. The inevitable break up came, but it wasn't just my girlfriend. I lost my friends too. I blamed myself a lot for not putting in enough effort to keep those relationships, but it really was like trying to keep a ship from sinking with only a bucket.

I cried more than I would like to admit. I cried in my bed, in the shower, in the bathroom, anywhere I could get some privacy. It got so bad that once my mother got upset and yelled at me to stop crying while I was in the shower. That hurt me, but after that I almost never cried again. Still, something felt broken inside of me. The academic aspect of school went great for me. I excelled in my classes. I got placed in English as a Second Language at first, but after one semester I was in regular English classes with my American peers. What became a motif was the struggle to fit in socially. The cafeteria was a nightmare. At first, I sat with the Mexican kids and other Hispanics, but they were completely different from my friends at Venezuela. I then sat with some Americans, but I couldn't keep up with their conversation. I could understand what they were saying but trying to chime in the conversation felt unnatural. By the time I thought of something to say and translated what I wanted to say from Spanish to English, they already moved on to another topic, so my remarks would land awkwardly. I became over conscious of how awkward I was being, which made me even more awkward and created a downward spiral. I've never felt more isolated than during those 30 minutes at lunch every day. I would often go to the restroom and spend as much time in there because at least being alone and enclosed in the four walls of the stall didn't make me feel as lonely as being in the sea of voices that I couldn't keep up with.

I should have joined some extracurricular activity to get out of my comfort zone. Instead, I got heavily into art since I was already good at it and didn't have to talk to anyone. Almost all my high school experience was focusing on classes, working hard on my art, avoiding people (especially at lunch), and then playing video games after school. I made a couple of friends with some of my classmates. To this day, my best friend, who I talk to pretty much every week, is a guy whom I met in geometry class during summer school. By the time I realized I shouldn't be avoiding people so much, I felt despair. I had underdeveloped social skills, so it seems like I was struggling to catch up to the people who always lived here and didn't go through what I went through. It was especially painful when I got crushes on girls but couldn't even find a way to get to know them.

Still, high school wasn't all suffering. I enjoyed the challenge of my classes and was satisfied at how self-reliant I became. I looked inward for comfort and found out how to appreciate solitude. High school came and went without much change. During senior year things began to change. I was more social, and much more hopeful than in previous years. Joining the after-school theater company made me realize just how much I was missing out on. Getting the first chance to go to homecoming and even a party was cut short by the pandemic. It was a bitter and twisted irony that as soon as I was coming out of my shell everyone was forced to become a cocoon and avoid everyone else.

So now I am attending college and I'm doing great. Luckily Mr. Dale hired me to work at Family Hope during the summer and it was an amazing opportunity. I got to help people and save enough money to also enroll in an EMT class. I got my EMT license, and I now work during the weekends in addition to also teaching physics three times a week.

What I am most grateful about living in America is the number of opportunities and choices that I have. It feels like I can become anything I want and that the only limiting factor is myself instead of any outside factors. It is a very motivating feeling that how far I get depends solely on how much work I put in. I want to become a PA (physician assistant) and won't stop until I get there.

REFLECTIONS: Kindness and Work

Kindness

I have heard it said and seen it in action, "Kindness costs nothing and means everything." These days, Venezuelans usually come with minimal of resources in their suitcases, but a wealth of kindness and skills. As doctors, lawyers and engineers flee from Venezuela and run to America for a better life, it is often referred to as a "brain drain" for Venezuela. While America benefits from their education and job skills, we are filled with gratitude for their contagious trait of kindness. Venezuelans have earned the reputation for their kindness throughout Latin America and now in America. When Andrea, a Venezuelan, came for assistance from Family Hope, she said very humbly and with kindness, "We have never had to ask for help before, but we just don't have enough money to pay the rent this month." Upon receiving help to avoid being evicted from her apartment, she shed tears of joy and continues to help other Venezuelans in similar situations. Through the tough days and now some very good days for Andrea, she radiates with kindness. When I saw face after face wait in their cars at Family Hope's Food Fair each month, I began to understand the level of kindness that somehow was innate to their being. It was not a smile of happiness for the moment, but a sincere feeling of being kind their whole life. This is the way they live! Another example is Julette, a young 24-year-old talented Venezuelan artist and illustrator of this book who now goes by Julie as a professional. An insurance company specifically hired Julette for her kindness as she is the voice for the company's call center, which receives calls from clients frustrated with their insurance plans. Julette's kind and pleasant voice often can bring a calm and a more positive viewpoint about the care and compassion of the company. However, do not misinterpret Julette's kindness as weakness. Rather, her kindness is wrapped with tough resilience, which is exactly what the company needs. If you are blessed to have a Venezuelan neighbor, expect to come to know a very kind friend. When I think of kindness, I think of Gledys and Rosangela who work with passion and joy to help people like Andrea and other Venezuelans receive adequate food and furniture to make a better life in America. Each Venezuelan coming to Family Hope seems to provide a face of kindness as they have carried this value with them to America. When you read some of the heartbreaking stories of these Venezuelans who had to flee for their lives, you may wonder why they are not consumed with anger? However, when I interviewed people like Rita, I heard the pain of the past, the tears of sadness, and the strong hope for a new life in America. Despite all the sadness, her story is painted with strokes of kindness and hope. Like Paul in Corinthians says, "Love is patient, love is kind…" (I Corinthians 13:4 NASB)

Henry, a businessman from Venezuela, admits that Venezuelans' instinct to be kind worked against them when it came time to protest the regime in the streets of Venezuela. It was not their nature to be this angry. As a result, the protests in Venezuela failed in 2016 and 2017 to demand a change in leadership. In fact, now life continues to become harder economically without much opposition from the people.

For me, I consider it a privilege to work and befriend hundreds of Venezuelans who have every reason to be angry with their government, and yet live with a kindness to others. I often asked, "Why did not more Venezuelans flood the streets when it came time to overthrow the regime?" Henry's story answers this question: "Venezuelans by nature are kind, and the violence needed in the streets to overthrow this corrupt government seemed in opposition to the garments of kindness they had worn all their lives."

You may ask, "Are not all cultures filled with kindness?" Throughout these pages, I emphasize that these are Venezuelan stories. I have met many kind cultures, and each showed a special nature of them to applaud. When I travel to other countries, I can always find special qualities that I admire about each one's history and the way they live. As for the Venezuelans, "kindness" fills their stories and their lives.

How can we become more kind? As Americans become more politically divided, we as Christians walk the fine line of speaking our convictions and living Jesus' command to love. Despite the zeal by First Century Christians to speak the truth, particularly against the Roman Government, the new Christians were primarily known for their love and their acts of mercy. For example, during a plague in Rome where sick people were left behind at Tiberian Isle, Christians stayed and cared for the sick when everyone else had abandoned them. In 1 Corinthians 13, the Apostle Paul defined love as "kindness" right after "patience." Whatever political brand you are, may you never lose sight of the major quality of a Christian...to love and to show kindness. When we enter political debate, we do not leave our Christ-like character at home. If you cannot treat your opponent as one to whom Jesus can show love to, then I suggest you refrain from any political dialogue. Just pray silently. Never underestimate the power of prayer to change hearts. We live in a culture where we feel a need to be in control and expect everyone to believe like we do. But that often breeds disharmony, unkind words and actions. Now with the advent of Artificial Intelligence, we will become more dependent on human and artificial ways to influence viewpoints to be more like us. In contrast to that line of thought, prayer can change attitudes regarding the life around us. We can be kind despite our circumstances.

I remember in November of 1989 when the Berlin Wall came down, dividing East and West Berlin. Days after the wall was down, I interviewed a university Lutheran professor from East Berlin who had witnessed this transformative time in history. He said, "Within all the calls to take down the wall, we should never forget how God's people witnessed to their convictions. For the past twelve months, every Sunday night, youth have been meeting for candlelight services to pray and to worship, calling upon God to tear down this wall. God answered our prayers!"

In our political rhetoric, may you be God's peacemaker willing to speak your convictions but still with the attitude of love and kindness to your neighbor. Isn't that a better way to treat our neighbor or one we have previously viewed as our political enemy? All those whom we walk and talk with deserve the same grace as we are given through our Lord Jesus Christ.

QUESTIONS:
1. In what areas of your life can you use more kindness?
2. Share about a time you regret not being more kind to someone.
3. Share or journal about someone hard to love in your life. How can you practice kindness?
4. How can you be more of a peacemaker in our world?
5. What can you learn from the Venezuelans?

Work

A modern version of an ancient story: The immigration officer in Miami asked a new Venezuelan two questions: "Who are you? What are you doing here?" The very smart Venezuelan responded: "How much do I need to pay you each month to ask me these two questions?" Most immigrants come with an enthusiasm to work and strive for a great purpose…to provide for their families and to begin the path to the American Dream. Currently, to work as a doctor in Venezuela might bring you $30/month in pay. In America, the opportunities for higher salaries will almost be guaranteed. I marveled at Venezuelans' willingness to work when they arrive in America. My friend, John, said to me, "I have mostly Venezuelans working for me. I love their work ethic!" When I referred these Venezuelans to other bosses, I would hear the same as CEO Matt's words, "Dale, find me more Venezuelans to hire." At first, I was not sure how some of the Venezuelans trained as doctors, lawyers and engineers would work at construction jobs, cleaning houses, and other jobs not in their profession. Quickly, I discovered the Venezuelans were willing to try almost any job to help their family succeed. They came with an entrepreneurial attitude and found ways to use their skills and savvy business experience to overcome any deficit. For example, Andreas, a former businessman in Venezuela, works in manufacturing from 8:30am to 5pm. Then from 6pm – 10pm drives a car to transport people. It is not only that Venezuelans are willing to accept any jobs, but they also work long hours to financially provide for their families. Remember, they make a choice of living in safe neighborhoods with excellent schools which often increases the family budget to afford additional rent. This work ethic resembles many immigrants coming to America in past generations who overcame language and cultural differences to succeed in America. The Venezuelan families of Gledys and Rosangela have worked long hours to afford new houses next door to each other to enjoy the safe neighborhood and provide the best education for their children. Many bosses and managers in Fort Bend County, Texas, have experienced and appreciated the work ethic of Venezuelans.

When you see the bus loads of immigrants dropped off in cities in America, know that even the most skilled and talented take five to eight years to fulfill some of their great dreams and purpose.

However, just like my great grandparents, it is not easy to begin a new life. It may take perseverance and years to buy a house after working very long days. For example, Jose' was a veterinarian in Venezuela. At first, he could not use his medical skills since they did not transfer into the American medical system. Instead, he became a high school science teacher. Not just any kind of teacher, but one year he received the highest honor of "Teacher of the Year" for his school district. Now after eight years in America with three children in college and a house, he will take his final Veterinarian Boards this spring and begin his love as a state certified Veterinarian. Dr. Jose' will tell you the whole process introduced him to many amazing Americans and produced greater purpose and character for his next journey.

We need a healthy system that treats these new immigrants with dignity and the freedom to discover the opportunities to work and thrive in America. Each one is created by God for a purpose. For all of us, native to the U.S. or new like Jose', we need to ask ourselves, "Who am I?" In other words, how is my identity shaping my choices? "What am I doing here?" Translated as, "What is my purpose? What is my calling in life?" No one can do it for us. These two questions are for each person's journey: Who are you? What are you doing here, or what is your purpose?

QUESTIONS:
1. How can you help or mentor someone else in guiding them to find their purpose?
2. At this season of your life's journey, answer the two questions: Who are you? What is your God-given purpose?
3. What can we learn from the Venezuelans?

"A TRIBUTE TO MY FATHER"

By Camilla

(13 year old Daughter of a Venezuelan Doctor who immigrated to the U.S., then contacted COVID-19 and died.)

My dad, "Tito": How can I describe such an amazing and special man like him? He was like the rainbow after a rainy day, or the shiny stars in the dark night sky. My dad meant everything to me. He was the most caring and supportive person I ever met.

I can't remember a time where he made me think that I couldn't do something that made me happy or that I wasn't capable of reaching my goals. He always encouraged me and my brothers to strive for the best versions of ourselves and never give up on our dreams, no matter what.

He did everything he could to make my mother feel like the most wonderful and special woman in the world. During the 12 years I spent with my dad, I learned so much. He was an extremely wise and intelligent man, and he made every day a new life lesson for us. I will always keep all the memories I shared with him in my heart, all the stories, all the jokes, all the happy moments we spent together.

I like to believe that everything happens for a reason. However, I can't help but think about how much I wish God had given me a little bit more time with my dad to be able to thank him for everything he did for me and my family. He deserves the whole world, and I just hope that wherever he is right now, he is happy. For me, he will always be the strongest fighter, the most courageous superhero, my role model, and just the best father anyone could ever wish for. I will do whatever it takes to achieve my number one goal which is to make my father proud. My dad will always be my favorite person and I will never love someone as much as him.

89

CHAPTER FOUR

Embracing Hope...Building a New Life

Jose' M

In 2021, we came with two children to the U.S. Why? We were looking for security. Our beloved country, Venezuela, was no longer safe to live and raise our children. We lived in Costa Rica for five years before coming to the U.S. We received notification filled with nonsense charges to appear in Venezuela. The Costa Rica authorities warned me that I could be deported to Venezuela. Therefore, we began planning our journey to America.

In 2013, the election of a new president began the great decline of Venezuela. I was in the intelligence of the police department. After the election, all the police were sent for training, and I would be sent to the most dangerous part of the country. The Director of police was appointed by the Government regime. He would have the same ideology as the government. This new direction would send officers to homes of people and put them in jail without any warning. I said to myself, "I can't do this anymore." I witnessed an 80-year-old woman beaten in the streets. Therefore, with the encouragement and support of very good friends, I resigned from the police force that had become so ruthless.

Now, a year later after moving to America, my kids are in school. Sometimes we become very anxious to know and recall all the corrupt ways of the Venezuelan government. However, we are looking forward. This is a safe place where kids can walk to school and not be afraid, and they receive an excellent education. We have learned it is not about things, but a peace in living in the best country in the world. We miss our country, but we know that we can never go back. We have found so many good people and help from churches and Family Hope. We know the value of work, so we are responsible and use all our skills to provide a good living for our family. We also want to help others in their lives. When you help, it doesn't mean you get something back. It is just the best way to live.

I tell my kids that it doesn't matter if we are rich or poor. We live by making the right decisions. Also, we believe and have experienced that God provides. After I paid all the expenses including flight to come to the U.S., I had $20. Now after a year, I have seen great opportunities come to me and my family. As for my family, we are a team. We work hard. We believe in family first. And we hold unto faith that God will always be by our side. We look back and see it was a great risk to come to the U.S. We now wonder, "How did we do it?" Only by God's grace, we are here, and we are rich with a new future and many opportunities. We are so grateful for you Americans who have been so generous!

Lopez

I arrived in this country with only my family as I crossed the Border. I was pregnant and all I had was the clothes that I was wearing. Amazing miracle occurred in that first year when I met Gledys from Family Hope. Her love, encouragement, words of strength and financial assistance helped us with shoes for my family, gift cards and clothes for the baby. I never imagined that America would be this generous to me. Mr. Dale is a great man with a good heart and kindness who is so willing to help people like me. These have been hard times for my family, but I discovered the Family Hope team was just one call away to give us a hand and tell us: "You can. Keep going! God is with you!"

As an undocumented immigrant, it is not easy to support yourself. However, Family Hope has opened its doors for us and many families to feel the love and presence of God. My two daughters and my husband will never forget the love shown to us!

Migdalys

I was a businesswoman with my husband in Venezuela. We worked for many years to build our company. Sadly, our business was taken over by the so-called government officials, leaving our business bankrupt. Every day we received threats. They shot bullets into our windows and destroyed our business. In view of this bad situation, we came through the Border over a year ago. We know what it is to work hard so we came to use our skills and good work experience to help our son and daughter. Sometimes I clean houses. My husband works construction with my son.

At my cleaning job, God blessed me with a friend who told me about Family Hope. They gave me school supplies, new shoes for my children, food, and clothes for my daughter. Today, we continue to fight for our economic stability and find a good job for my husband. We have already applied for Asylum and are waiting for God's timing to complete the process. During this waiting period, my husband had to leave to work at a better job in another state. I look forward to the time when my wonderful husband and I will be reunited. It is not easy to live apart like this, but I know that nothing is impossible in this country. This country is full of blessings, and we will succeed. Family Hope, we will never be able to repay you for everything you have done for all my Venezuelan brothers and sisters. We are very good and hard-working people. We will continue to do our best at our lives in America. Thanks for all the blessings we have received.

Zahira

I am a wife and mother of three beautiful princesses. I was an Industrial Engineer in Venezuela and worked 18 years in the oil industry. In 2021, we had to leave a lifetime behind without knowing what was yet to come. We left our house, turned off the lights, closed the door, my husband and hugged each other while crying and with faith in God, took a backpack to travel to the U.S. When we arrived in Katy, TX, we went to St. Faustina Church, Fulshear, TX. We received a generous welcome from them, and then they sent us to Family Hope which was only a few blocks away. I still remember meeting Rosangela and Gledys of Family Hope. They gave us food, but more importantly HOPE that we can make it in this country. I made a beautiful cake for Mr. Dale for the noble work you have achieved for all of us coming to America with so many needs. This cake was really a celebration for all the families who come to this country with their suitcases full of dreams and hopes. Family Hope, you are our angel with generous hearts to change our world.

Eva

I was born in Venezuela. I graduated from the university as a Public Accountant. I worked for 16 years as a supervisor in a business. My husband and I are parents to a boy 9 years old. We decided to embark on a new path to the United States since our dream is that our son can have the best education.

We arrived in 2021 through the border without money or property. We experienced many moments of anguish and worries. When we finally came to Katy, TX, my husband's sister told us about a non-profit institution called Family Hope. Gledys invited me to attend a class for parents called, "Raising Highly Capable Kids."

Through Family Hope, we have met some very good people who have a pure soul. They have always been there for us. We are givers and want to give back, so we volunteer at Family Hope to help others who are in our shoes. Family Hope, as the name says, is a great family of HOPE and a team to support so many people. We are on the path of a better future in this country. My infinite gratitude to God for putting so many people in our path to help us and bless us.

Martin

On December 2019, my husband and I boarded a plane for the USA as we had planned for several months. We landed in Miami and then we flew to our long-awaited destination in Houston. We could not wait to hug our grandson, daughter and son-in-law who had traveled to America a year before. Our plan was to share the holidays with them and return in January. However, God had other plans. On our way back while we were in the airport of Miami, our daughter called us and said, "Mommy, Daddy, it's your time to go back because they closed all the borders in Venezuela due to the Pandemic." We could not believe it, but we called relatives in Venezuela, and they assured us it was true.

Thinking it was something temporary, we left our bags at a friend's house in Miami and returned to Texas. Days, weeks, months passed without being able to do anything to return to Venezuela. Our passports and visas expired. We cried a lot knowing that Venezuela had serious difficulties of theft, kidnapping and extortion. As a result, we were in a new country without much money.

Faced with this new reality, we said, "Yes, we have to stay, and we must do everything legally." We requested an extension to our stay. After the extension, we accepted asylum. We obtained a blessing of being favored in the last lottery of visas in which Venezuela participated.

Living in this country has allowed us to bear witness to the love of God in our lives and God's great purpose for us. Valuable human beings gave us support at just the right time such as Gledys and Rosangela of Family Hope. In the face of doubts and worry, a wonderful organization called Family Hope provided food that minimized the economic impact.

We thank God because we are with family under one roof. My husband required an urgent heart operation, and everything went perfectly. He has now recovered. We have obtained legal documents, and now we can work. We have experienced angels who have extended their hand to us and welcomed us to this great country. We say thank you to Family Hope. At a Christmas party for all of us in need, Santa Claus and assistants gave my grandson a gift. He was so happy because none of us had much money to buy Christmas gifts. It was an experience so spectacular. When you have so little, these gestures fill our soul with infinite thanks.

Maria B

I worked for 20 years at a company of public accountants in Venezuela dedicated to the collections of municipal taxes. The main reason I came to America was to seek a cure for my son who had been suffering from a medical condition for three years. He had been treated by more than 25 specialists in Venezuela without any improvement. In America, we found the needed care that we were seeking. Slowly my son improved. Certainly, the language and customs were difficult barriers, but the saddest part was missing my family and the businesses we worked at for years.

Today, we are here in America, thanks to the charity of many people and the discovery of our talents and new opportunities. I believe God sent angels along the way to assist my family. My greatest joy is to see my son healthy, safe, and happy with a bright future full of opportunities for him and for us. I am now becoming better at English. My husband and I are advancing in our jobs and receiving approvals for our immigration process. I no longer feel alone, but so grateful.

Geidy

I was born in Venezuela and married for 25 years. I was a Dentist for more than 20 years of experience. We were forced to immigrate to America because we saw our country changing for the worst. We were seeking a good quality of life and more opportunities for our children. It was a very drastic decision, but we arrived in America three years ago with our lives packed in a suitcase with fears, a lot of uncertainty, and great hope. I don't know how we would have ever made our transition in America without Family Hope who always did what their name said...HOPE. They gave us love and lots of faith with unconditional help and multiple donations of food. God bless Family Hope who was a shining light to protect us and guide us into a new life. We are eternally grateful!

Gladys

I am from Venezuela. A year ago, I came to the U.S.A., like thousands of brothers and sisters looking to improve our quality of life. We came with our suitcases full of dreams, lacking many things, but always believing that God would send wonderful people into our midst and bless us. I remember the day when Family Hope came with their truck and brought furniture to our almost empty apartment. Before this time, we were sleeping on the floor. Along with the furniture, we were provided with food and clothes for our school-age children. We are so grateful for Mr. Dale of Family Hope, a gentleman with a kind heart and a beautiful smile to help all of us in need. Throughout this time, I have witnessed so many kind and generous people willing to help. When we first came to America, I wondered if we would be alone to figure out all the new ways of living. I was pleasantly surprised. With our connections to Family Hope and many friends, our journey has been supported by the best people at just the right time. Thank you, America, for letting us be part of your great country!

Yesika

I am from Venezuela, and I worked at the electric company. We decided to come to America because we did not agree with the political thinking of the president. Our first months in the U.S.A. were difficult due to the sudden changes of language and culture. But, thanks to the help of good people along the way, we have experienced amazing opportunities that this country offers everyone.

Family Hope was a shining star in our days of wondering if we would make it. They gave us both food and guidance in finding resources to keep our hopes alive. Despite the hardships, this is a country that gives you everything. You must follow the laws and dedicate yourself to working hard, but we have a roof over our heads to sleep and eat. We are safe and don't miss the bad ways of the Venezuelan officials, but we miss our country, our roots, and family.

I am convinced that we made the right decision. We feel positive things about adapting to the American way of life. I pray to God to take care of our family and give us wisdom and patience to keep learning a new language and adapt to the economic system in America. I know this country offers us all the necessary opportunities we need to have a full life.

Young Maria

My name is Maria, I am 10 years old. I have been in the United States for 6 years. I started gymnastics in Venezuela at the age of 3. When I was 4 years old, my family decided to move to the United States. After a year in the United States, my mother decided to enroll me in Westwood Gymnastics in Katy, TX, where I was part of the academy for only two years. Because the pandemic began in 2019, we had to take security measures, and that is when I decided to change my academy. In October 2021, I attended a new academy in Katy, TX. During this time, I did a backhand spring in which I made a bad move and fractured my left wrist. I went to the hospital, and they gave me a splinter to recover the fracture. I got therapy for 2 months. After 2 months, they put me in a cast, and I was in a cast for 4 weeks, Eventually, they put an orthopedic device on me to help heal the wound. I am a very good student, and I received an invitation for this summer to go to the Academy National Youth Leadership in Houston. However, I cannot attend because my parents don't have enough money for me to go this summer. Because I participate in the World Champions Center academy directed by Simone Biles, I dream of becoming an Olympic gymnast representing the United States even though in my heart I am still proud to be born in Venezuela. I thank the

United States for giving me so many opportunities to achieve all my dreams and goals.

Laura

We are a Venezuelan family experiencing blessings of all kinds and always overcoming obstacles. My husband was a Mechanical Engineer and worked in the Venezuelan oil industry for 18 years. I was a History and Geography teacher with a great passion for educating young people by showing them our roots, culture, space, and infinite stories that shape our towns, cities and countries. We have three children.

Suddenly, our beautiful country of Venezuela began to regress. Nothing was going well anymore. The children who attended music, dance, English and sports classes began to run out of teachers. Many of the teachers immigrated to other countries. Venezuela was decadent without gasoline and without electricity. It became very difficult when the oil companies closed their doors leaving thousands of people unemployed.

In December 2022, we arrived in the U.S. with a single suitcase full of dreams. Friends and acquaintances gave us guidelines on how to establish ourselves in America. The first night we moved into an apartment in Texas, Family Hope was present. We were greeted with big smiles, giving us encouragement and great support with clothes for the cold weather, toys for the children, furniture, and generous hearts to let us know that we would not be alone. Since then, our children have adapted satisfactorily to the school system and receive excellent grades. We hope to provide additional classes of music for our children who love to play the flute. They also play soccer and want to learn to be proficient in languages.

We work hard every day. We know that to achieve our goals, we must fight for them. We will achieve these purposes and create stability for our children. Though we have a lot to learn about this great country and culture, God has a big heart to bless us and be faithful to us.

Family Hope has been a blessing to us. In the future, we want to repay them for the great support by offering our services, knowledge, humility, work, values, and good customs. We intend to respect the culture of those who opened the doors for us to start over and show how God has provided so much. We are proud to live in America!

Joscellym

Leaving your home country for the first time in the middle of a political controversy as an immigrant is a very hard act. I am currently the mother of two teenagers. We arrived in the United States in December 2016 with only three suitcases, personal documents, mixed feelings of sadness and hope, plus many ideas of how it would be to start a new life in the wonderful city of Houston. We came to live in Texas thanks to the references of friends who received us here the first days while we were settling in. Upon arrival, we realized that Houston is very similar to our hometown in Venezuela, Maracaibo: People are very rooted in their culture, very helpful, very regionalist, very loving of their idiosyncrasy, enterprising, being kind and genuine when it comes to lend a helping hand. We arrived with only $300 dollars in our hands after expenses, eager to grow and work to continue our lives in this country. Soon we were blessed to receive the help of Family Hope with a first English course that they offered to the immigrant community. For me, this was a first step to getting to know a beautiful community. Our classes started at 6 pm in their offices, and these were my first small steps in learning a new language. But I assure you that it was not all about the classes.

I met Mr. Dale and his wife, Alene, who really had true service to the immigrant community. They were angels on earth! Mr. Olson, whom I currently consider part of my family in Texas, is a wonderful man who God endowed with his best attributes because he works with excellence for the service of the neediest, dedicated to help and provide solutions without any hesitation and without any qualms is an unwavering person of soul. I am certain that he has a gift of service to people that I seldom see in other people. His actions through the years of service with Family Hope are reflected in more than 41,000 happy families receiving his humanitarian actions each year. Mr. Dale, in conjunction with his team, accomplished impressive goals to bless entire families in this very hard process of being an immigrant. Personally, I have witnessed this while I had the privilege of working alongside him in the social media communication strategies and sharing videos of the food fairs that took place, sometimes in the harshest and most inclement weather. For Mr. Dale, the wind, the rain or the strong heat never erased his characteristic smile, his words of encouragement and his prayers of blessing of the day for the volunteer team before each food fair. He is the reflection of a great human being who works tirelessly to serve all in need.

Ivanna

I have two children, ages 2 and 14 years old. I was an Anesthesiologist in Venezuela. My husband was also a doctor. Because the government seemed to be always checking on our personal and professional work, my husband and I decided to go to Peru and work. I left my daughter with my grandparents. While in Peru, I became pregnant, so I went back to Venezuela to have the baby. However, my baby was born prematurely and died nine hours later. My feeling was that they did not use the right medication at the hospital for my situation. Ten days later, I returned to Peru while my daughter continued to stay with her grandparents.

Did I ever fear the government? I always had an uneasy feeling when government officials came to the hospital or other places of work. Personally, I was not threatened, but I know colleagues who were very fearful and felt threatened. We never knew when the government officials might take action against us.

While I was in Peru, I became pregnant again, and she was a beautiful girl. She was ten months old when we decided to come to the United States. Since we did not feel safe in Peru and experienced an unstable economy, we made our big decision to fly from Lima, Peru to Columbia to Mexico City to Monterey. From Monterey, we were given a ride of six hours until we reached the river and finally crossed into America.

Since we had family in New Jersey, we flew to New Jersey to stay one and a half months. Then, we flew to Houston to be close to other family members. We are so glad to live in a safe neighborhood in Katy, TX.

The most difficult part of our time in America was the language barrier. I am learning English, but I have not mastered the language yet. I have a work permit, and I am surprised by the work opportunities in America. This is different than Peru where they were worried that Venezuelans would take their jobs.

I am grateful for the safe feeling in America. Even the laws to drive a car are obeyed in the U.S., unlike the unruly traffic in Venezuela. I believe that if we work hard in the U.S., we will be able to improve the quality of our life. Someday, I will master English, and then I will have even more opportunities. My daughter gives me a perspective at times when I get frustrated and say, "I think I am going back to Venezuela." My daughter responds, "Mommy, I am staying here. I love it. I love my school. I love this neighborhood." I know that someday, I will return to the medical field and become re-certified in my field. We are glad to be in this safe country with a stable economy. I know our future is bright!

When I look ahead five years, my hopes and dreams are that my children will have a better life, will learn English, and live in this great place with so many opportunities for a good quality of life. I am especially grateful that I can send my child outside and know they will not be kidnapped or fear any violence against them. My only fear living in America is when I hear someone shooting weapons in a school, which reminds me of the violence back home in Venezuela. I have a very magical feeling knowing that my children will be better by living in the U.S. The one word is "opportunities." This is a land filled with opportunities. It is just like when we vacationed here in America. We have seen movies from America. Venezuelans love music, and we love the talent in America. We have always considered America "amazing" and filled with potential. As you can tell, we love America!

REFLECTIONS: Hope

"Therefore, if anyone is in Christ, they are a new creation; the old has passed away; behold, new things have come." (2 Corinthians 5:17 NASB) Most of the Venezuelans I meet come with a faith in Jesus Christ. They do not naively expect God to fix all their worries, but they do pray to God for strength to face all the challenges as a new immigrant in America. One year we hosted a Christmas celebration at our house, and I remember holding the one-month-old daughter of Angelica, who had just come to the U.S. in the past two months. As she wrote in her story, they came with a greater hope for a new life for their children, and a faith that Christ would provide and bless them. At the time, they would never have predicted how tough life would unfold with three children, finding jobs to support their family, and drawing strength emotionally from God to persevere in learning English in this new culture. Yet, in all those days of wonder, she would be at Family Hope's Food Fair alongside so many Venezuelans volunteering so others would be served food.

Local churches generously responded to the kindness of the Venezuelans and their support has been essential to Family Hope's outreach to the community. For example, Second Baptist Church, sponsored a Christmas event and brought 40 people by bus to the church. On the bus, I met Maria and her daughter who had been in the U.S. less than two weeks. To this day, she has a great memory and appreciation for the food, inspiring Christmas message, and the generous gifts given to her daughter that night. For her, it was an amazing beginning in America…a sign that God who came down in love as Jesus would love her in this new life in Katy,

Texas. At that time, she had no idea that in the coming year she would meet her future husband and give birth to their new son.

Another local church, St. Faustina Catholic Church added an extra food fair each month and sends food monthly to parishes in Venezuela. I came to know Isabel and Jose' through an organization called "Pounds of Love." These very dedicated people of God receive donations to buy the food, pack the food in boxes monthly, and send over 2,000 pounds a month to feed families who are nearly starving in Venezuela. Truly, this is faith and hope in action!

When faith inspires deeds of love and acts of mercy, we touch lives in profound ways that can transform lives. We become the hands and feet of Jesus. I think of the woman who anointed Jesus with precious oils prior to Jesus riding into Jerusalem on the week of Passover. Being anointed by the woman now gave a new credence of smelling like a king as he rode down the streets of Jerusalem and the people responded, "Hosanna! Son of David!" Similarly, when our faith inspires us to share beautiful acts of mercy like sending boxes of food to a starving country or to carry bags of fresh fruits, vegetables, rice and pasta into a car for a neighbor in need of food, so our whole being and the air we breathe radiate the living hope of Christ, our Savior. Hope has a way of keeping people alive! We can be the light! I urge you to find ways to give people HOPE in the name of Christ.

Never underestimate the power in an act of mercy. I remember meeting Camilla, who shared her tribute of her father. Her father had just died of COVID a month after coming to the U.S. Now it was only her mother and two brothers during the first Christmas in America. She was a seventh grader with dreams of becoming a tennis star. One problem, joining the tennis team meant she needed a tennis racket which she had to leave back in Venezuela. She also wanted to learn to play piano. Two families related to

Family Hope made this Christmas special for her, one that she would never forget. On Christmas morning, my wife and I came to her apartment with a tennis racket from a mother who had three girls in tennis and a new keyboard from a couple who just loved to give. Camilla was in awe as she received these two gifts on Christmas morning! The tears of joy shared in the mixture of losing a father and the fears of living with only the basics in America. We were their first visitors even though they had lived in their apartment for six months. By the warm welcome we received, we realized they must have felt alone in this new country. That Christmas morning, my wife and I shared the love of Jesus through the gift of HOPE… for a new beginning in America. All things are possible with God! Since then, she has been a star on her tennis team and an amazing student with a new hope.

How is God calling you to bring HOPE to someone who really needs you? Our country was founded on neighbors reaching out and walking beside each other as loving bearers of hope.

QUESTIONS:
1. How can you bring greater hope to your neighbor or someone in need?
2. Recall a season in your life that seemed void of hope, and someone befriended you to shine a new reason to live.
3. How can we learn from the Venezuelans?

CHAPTER FIVE

Family Hope

FAMILY HOPE…a place where people can come to receive compassion, be given resources to improve their life, and hope is found.

In 2015, Family Hope began sponsoring food fairs for the community by the support of Houston Food Bank and Second Mile (a larger non-profit organization) at three church parking lots, River Bend Baptist Church, Zion Chapel Missionary Baptist Church, and Parkway Fellowship. I am especially grateful to the Houston Food Bank's requirement that ALL people who attend are served at these Food Fairs. When 100 – 200 volunteers would come to participate at a food fair, I always encouraged them to put on "eyes of grace." I said, "Today, you have one job: To serve your neighbor!" As I greeted families with children and some grandparents in car after car in the church parking lot and then proceed in line with their trunks open to receive bags of healthy food from a volunteer, I said to myself: "What are their stories? Certainly, each face must have a story of sadness and tough days. Some have been waiting in line for two hours to receive food so will these items of vegetables, fruit and canned items be enough to sustain them until next month?" As I came to know each family who came for help, I discovered many had the grit to persevere through difficult times and succeed in life. But with rising costs, their looming question each month was, "Can I pay the rent for our apartment?" While volunteers would arrive at the food fairs at 7am, Venezuelans created a norm of parking at 5:30am, waiting to be the first to receive food so they could later go to work. I would question why they chose to live where apartment rent was higher than other parts of Houston. As I came to hear their stories, I began to understand their values: They came to America to live in a safe neighborhood and have the best schools for their children, even if it meant working two jobs and attending food fairs like Family Hope to sustain them. As a result, after nine years of sharing life with the Venezuelan community and feeding over 40,000 individuals a year and giving away over 1,000 new pairs of shoes before the beginning of school, they were quick to tell their new friends to come to Family Hope. In the earlier years, they arrived legally waiting for their meeting to claim "Asylum." Today with the southern border wide open, migrants arrive from Venezuela and numerous countries weekly. More recently, some Venezuelans coming through the southern border were told, "Make your first stop at Family Hope. They will be your friends to help you!"

I encourage you to support your local charity. In every community, the need is greater than their resources. On the walls of Family Hope, you will see the words of wisdom from Mother Sister Teresa that give us a barometer of conscience to love our neighbor with charitable words and actions.

No non-profit has enough resources to pay families' rent month after month. How do you decide who receives help? As CEO of Family Hope, I had to make tough decisions in being a good steward of donations given to us. My goal was to help as many families as possible. No one family could receive everything. If my staff and I gave too much, they became dependent and lacked the entrepreneurial spirit to work and learn the skill of perseverance that they needed in the long run. Family Hope was founded on helping people who were in a season of emergencies and great need. However, from the beginning, we understood the two sides of healthy helping: 1) In Emergencies, for food, rent and medical needs. 2) Equipping families with skills to improve their lives such as Parenting Classes, Financial classes, Healthy Cooking Class, and connecting individuals to job opportunities.

Regarding EMERGENCY need, I remember a one-time unique request from Antonio, a new Venezuelan café' owner, who came to me for help. He could not pay the rent for his new business of less than a year old. It was unusual to receive a request for a business owner seeking help from Family Hope to survive. After hearing his story and knowing of his business, Family Hope took a big risk and helped him. Today, he tells other people, "It was this gift of kindness from Family Hope that made all the difference, and he emphatically insists that gift was a turning point for his restaurant. Today, his business is flourishing, and Antonio is giving back to Family Hope! Of course, I can tell you hundreds of stories of people being helped by Family Hope so they could avoid being evicted from their apartment or relieved of some of their medical debt. Helping people during emergencies gives second chances to improve their lives and give back!

On the EQUIPPING side, I began to see the Venezuelans coming to our popular parent class, "Raising Highly Capable Kids." The parenting class is built on the work of Search Institute of Minneapolis, Minnesota which asked the question: "What are the core assets needed by high school students to succeed?" As a result, *Raising Highly Capable Kids* published by Rezilient Kidz based its curriculum on 40 Assets needed for parents to train their children. Some of the 40 Assets include, "Responsibility...Serving others...Communication...Having another nurturing adult in their life." At first, I wondered if the Venezuelans needed this course. However, I quickly began to receive positive feedback from the Venezuelans for the information in the class. I realized *Raising Highly Capable Kids* was an effective parenting course as well as a summary of citizenship in America. We should never underestimate the need for new people to our country to learn about American values and principles to live together. Ask any CEO about the need for new employees to attend business training, and they will speak passionately about all employees knowing and affirming the same values and principles expected. I am now hearing from the first Venezuelans who have become citizens. They are proud of not only being an American but feel grateful for the opportunity to study American history and values. Together with the teaching of the 40 Assets from the parent class, they are more informed and healthier citizens.

Family Hope's Financial Management classes were essential to the success of assimilating into the American culture. Ask winners of lotteries who had no money management skills. They could tell you the sorry story of burning through millions of dollars in a few short months because they had no guidance for money management skills. The Financial Management classes taught them to prioritize their expenses and to create a plan to achieve their goals. Non-profits, businesses, governments, CEO's and politicians, let us seek to teach a wise balance to money management…to be the best stewards of money…no matter how large or small the funds.

Another popular class offered by Family Hope was a cooking class taught in Spanish. When families first come to America, they are amazed at the multiple choices of foods, some healthier than others. Many immigrants gain weight because of the consumption of unhealthy foods in their diet. As a result, our chef, Lisette from Venezuela, teaches (via Zoom) ways to prepare healthy foods for their household. After two years of offering this class, participants include new families to America plus people living in Peru, Columbia, Venezuela and other Latin American countries.

Family Hope remains today as a place of COMPASSION and TRANSFORMATION. I consider it a privilege to be the founding CEO for Family Hope, and together with a caring staff and willing volunteers, we served so many people in need, coming from the community and countries around the world. However, a majority of those served in the last few years have been from Venezuela.

The kindness of Venezuelans touched our hearts as they wrapped their loving arms around Alene, my wife, and me with their special traditions and delicious food to celebrate our bond together. I was invited to birthday parties, First Communion ceremonies, baptisms, weddings and even hospital rooms as our database grew into the hundreds of Venezuelans connected to Family Hope. I am grateful for the area churches and amazing pastors who opened their doors to these new neighbors. They provided space for Family Hope Food Fairs, welcomed Venezuelans in worship and sponsored events to share faith together. Churches like Parkway Fellowship and St. Faustina who hosted food fairs often added gift cards to the grocery bags as their outreach of kindness. For the many donors and citizens of the northern Fort Bend County of Texas, I am grateful for their generous donations of time and funds to reach out to our Venezuelan neighbors so they might have a better life in America. Thank you to every person, business, and organization who continues with joy to serve their neighbors!

In conclusion, I believe every face has a story. Just like diamonds, the Venezuelans are gems, so don't miss them. See the beauty in them and take time to learn from them. To all the Venezuelans who might read this book, "Welcome to America. We are a richer country by your presence. May we work together to bring a bright future to this country we love."

WAYS TO PARTICIPATE IN HELPING VENEZUELANS:

1. Support your local food shelf in your community through financial gifts and volunteer to help. You will be the one who will discover how blessed you are.

2. Host a parenting class, "Raising Highly Capable Kids," by Reszilent Kidz. Contact Family Hope for excellent speakers and training. The need is great for more parent training.

3. Give a financial gift to support the ongoing outreach to the Venezuelan community. www.familyhopefulshear.org (Fulshear Outreach and Development, DBA: Family Hope). This fund is intended to bring practical assistance to Venezuelans in this new country. (Family Hope is a 501 c3 organization. Originally it was called Fulshear Outreach and Development: EIN# 30-23417. Website: www.familyhopefulshear.org)

4. Welcome a new neighbor! You may be the first one to give them a warm welcome. There are multiple blessings in welcoming a new neighbor! This is the American way!

ACKNOWLEDGEMENTS

My sincere thanks to Alene, my wife, for her constant love, careful editing, and managing all the details leading to publishing.

Thanks to God for the inspiration to collect these Venezuelan stories and reflections.

A special thanks to Julie Ostos for her creative, beautiful artwork.

Thank you to Colt Melrose, for his amazing photography.

I am grateful for all the special Venezuelans who were willing to share their stories.

Thanks to the Family Hope staff: Gledys Pulgar, Rosangela D'cesar, Juan Palomares, Maria Nunez, Isabel Gonzales, Carolyn & Carlos Gonzales, Elsa Camero, Lisette Ostos.

Thanks to Bob Patton, President of Family Hope, and faithful friend.

My special thanks to the pastors in the northern Fort Bend County, Texas: Dr. Charles Wisdom, Mike McGown, Heath Pressley, Brian Brunke, Will Tucker, John Crowe, Steve Littlefield, Chris Saulnier, Kenny Johnson, Donnie Johnson, Jackie Gilmore, Bill Hogan, Josh Cullen, Kyle Leak, Nolan Donald and Father Dat.

I am so grateful for the teachers of the popular parenting class, "Raising Highly Capable Kids:" Linda Newsome Johnson, Bill Hogan and Translator, Maria Lossada.

A special thank you to the faithful leaders of Family Hope: Bob Patton, Chris Dibler, Mimi Harris, Erika Yelverton, and Bob Blue.

Thanks to the special community friends, John & Diane Hovas, Matt Fuhrman, Richard Caldwell & Barbara Stuckey, Tricia Krenek, Don McCoy, Red Warner, Blair Morrow, Kent Harris, Sandra Irish., Curt & Debbie Long, Bill & Marlene Oldham, Kathy Patton, John Warner, Michael Roberts, Lindy Melrose, Marcia Simmons, Bill Brothers, Laura & Don Ballard, Kellie Messer, Kevin Wann, Andrew Leeper, Anthony Dekker, Antonio & Martha Urdaneta, Deacon Rey and Brazos River Rotary friends.

I consider it a privilege to call Pastors James Giannantonio and Stephen Kelly my friends and theological mentors.

Thanks to Isabel & Jose' Sanabria and the volunteers of "Pounds of Love" for their big hearts to serve Venezuelans.

Thanks to Benny Irish & Katie Smith for their encouragement in the publishing process.

I am so grateful for the amazing leaders of northern Fort Bend County generously volunteered at food fairs and donated to Family Hope.

Thanks to the senior men golfers in Weston Lakes who have a generous heart to serve Family Hope.

Thanks to Sherry Eberle and Matt Leffel at Walmart for your generous donations to Family Hope.

Thanks to Sarah White from Second Mile who has been a friend and mentor.

Thanks to Quynh-Anh McMahan from The George Foundation, who even in the early years believed in Family Hope.

My thanks to former Mayor Kuykendall and Mayor Groff for your support of Family Hope.

I am grateful for my pastor, Jennifer Michael, who gives me spiritual nourishment.

Thanks to God for our children, Erik, Paul, and Lenea and their families whose love blesses our lives.

My thanks to the amazing Venezuelan community who inspired me and have shown kindness and love to Alene and me.

118

Made in the USA
Columbia, SC
22 June 2023

18641337R00065